Cambridge Elements

Elements in Eighteenth-Century Connections
edited by
Eve Tavor Bannet
University of Oklahoma
Markman Ellis
Queen Mary University of London

THE LONDON FOUNDLING HOSPITAL AND EIGHTEENTH-CENTURY OBJECTS OF CHARITY

Recovering the Digital Archive

Hilary E. Wyss
Trinity College

CAMBRIDGE
UNIVERSITY PRESS

Shaftesbury Road, Cambridge CB2 8EA, United Kingdom

One Liberty Plaza, 20th Floor, New York, NY 10006, USA

477 Williamstown Road, Port Melbourne, VIC 3207, Australia

314–321, 3rd Floor, Plot 3, Splendor Forum, Jasola District Centre, New Delhi – 110025, India

103 Penang Road, #05–06/07, Visioncrest Commercial, Singapore 238467

Cambridge University Press is part of Cambridge University Press & Assessment, a department of the University of Cambridge.

We share the University's mission to contribute to society through the pursuit of education, learning and research at the highest international levels of excellence.

www.cambridge.org
Information on this title: www.cambridge.org/9781009459914

DOI: 10.1017/9781009459891

© Hilary E. Wyss 2025

This publication is in copyright. Subject to statutory exception and to the provisions of relevant collective licensing agreements, no reproduction of any part may take place without the written permission of Cambridge University Press & Assessment.

When citing this work, please include a reference to the DOI 10.1017/9781009459891

First published 2025

A catalogue record for this publication is available from the British Library

ISBN 978-1-009-45991-4 Hardback
ISBN 978-1-009-45990-7 Paperback
ISSN 2632-5578 (online)
ISSN 2632-556X (print)

Cambridge University Press & Assessment has no responsibility for the persistence or accuracy of URLs for external or third-party internet websites referred to in this publication and does not guarantee that any content on such websites is, or will remain, accurate or appropriate.

For EU product safety concerns, contact us at Calle de José Abascal, 56, 1°, 28003 Madrid, Spain, or email eugpsr@cambridge.org

The London Foundling Hospital and Eighteenth-Century Objects of Charity

Recovering the Digital Archive

Elements in Eighteenth-Century Connections

DOI: 10.1017/9781009459891
First published online: December 2025

Hilary E. Wyss
Trinity College

Author for correspondence: Hilary E. Wyss, hilary.wyss@trincoll.edu

Abstract: The Foundling Hospital was established in London in 1739 to save impoverished infants from destitution and abandonment by separating them from their mothers and raising them in an institutional setting. The Hospital, which also housed an art collection, concert series, and fashionable park, became a monument to the largess of the benefactors willing to support the reshaping of supposedly unwanted babies into "worthy" citizens useful to their nation. In 2024, the Coram Foundation digitized parts of its voluminous archive from the eighteenth and nineteenth centuries, making these records available to the public in unprecedented ways. Through a close examination of the material artifacts of the Hospital, this analysis of the first few decades of this institution makes visible the uneasy tension between the perspective of the benefactors and the experiences of foundlings from the moment of separation from their birth parent(s) through their years associated with the Foundling Hospital.

Keywords: benevolence (charity), childhood, archive, Foundling Hospital, Thomas Coram

© Hilary E. Wyss 2025

ISBNs: 9781009459914 (HB), 9781009459907 (PB), 9781009459891 (OC)
ISSNs: 2632-5578 (online), 2632-556X (print)

Contents

	Introduction	1
1	Reception Day	14
2	Foundlings	41
	Conclusion	64
	Works Cited	71

Introduction

In 1739, Thomas Coram secured a royal charter for the Hospital for the Maintenance and Education of Exposed and Deserted Young Children, familiarly known as the Foundling Hospital. This London institution was an extraordinary venture, one that not only shaped English benevolence directed toward children for years to come, but also in many ways reshaped parenting, childhood, and authority in the eighteenth century. Captain Coram, as he was known for his long career in the sea trade, had become interested in the idea of a foundling hospital through his dismay at the terrible spectacle of impoverished babies and children seen on the streets of London, a dismay shared widely in the culture.[1] The Foundling Hospital took as its guiding principle that such children were best separated from their improvident mothers and raised in a rigidly controlled and documented institutional setting. Upon entry, the infant's age and gender were recorded on a form called a billet and then transferred into a volume called the General Register, where the child was identified by a number and a new name. From that point on the child was a "foundling" under the care of the institution, with every aspect of her/his life managed and documented in a series of registers. In this setting, child-rearing was reconceived as a masculinized form of recordkeeping, while the maternal and emotive elements of care were restructured as forms of labor assigned a specific monetary value. Perhaps even more significantly, the wrenching separation of infants from their mothers, so essential to the conception of the institution, was rendered not only palatable, but even desirable.

In October 2024, the Coram Foundation, which is the modern incarnation of the institution once known as the Foundling Hospital, digitized parts of its voluminous archive from the eighteenth and nineteenth centuries. The original archive, housed in The London Archive, is enormous; its catalogue list alone runs more than 800 pages and it covers a span of time from the early eighteenth century to the mid twentieth century. The digital archive covers a mere 23 percent of this material, but its focus on the earlier period (eighteenth and nineteenth centuries) and its extremely helpful historical apparatus make what was an unwieldy and dense archive available to modern readers in unprecedented ways. While the Coram Foundation today has come a long way from the institutional framework of the eighteenth century, it has maintained throughout

---

[1] This concern is dramatized in William Hogarth's famous 1751 print "Gin Lane," which shows a syphilitic and alcoholic mother dropping her baby off a bridge while reaching for a pinch of snuff. In the background, a young woman is buried while her child cries in front of the coffin. While this is intended as a study of the effects of gin, the central image is an improvident mother, suggesting the ways poverty and its effects on children were focused on women. Hogarth, not incidentally, was a strong supporter of the Foundling Hospital.

the centuries an abiding concern for the safety and care of children. Its commitment to the records of its past as well as its striving toward a better future have made this Element possible, even if the conclusions contained within it are very much my own.

This Element is designed to provide insight into some of the questions and issues made visible by the extraordinary set of documents newly accessible to the general public. By linking to specific records in this digital archive, I offer a close reading of the texts surrounding this venture – including the fragmentary words and instructions left by the mothers for their babies at the first stage of this institution (1741–56), the first fifteen years before the period known as the General Reception. By focusing on a relatively narrow period of the Hospital's 200-year existence (it took in children well into the twentieth century), I hope to focus on the principles and practices that shaped the institution at its founding in the mid eighteenth century before the many sweeping changes in the national and international scenes that affected the Hospital over its centuries of existence. By doing so, I make visible the connection between this London organization and the broader dynamics of charity and benevolence across the British Empire toward people (in this case children) understood as worthy of care. The notion of "worthiness" called forth extraordinary acts of benevolence, but at the same time justified and rationalized systemic suffering on a massive scale for those who were not seen as meriting the label. The Foundling Hospital embodied both sides of this terrible equation.

My intention is not to write an institutional history; there are already several well-regarded full-length publications related to the Foundling Hospital, and I am indebted to their analysis. Most recently Helen Berry's *Orphans of Empire* argues for the central place of the Foundling Hospital in Britain's growing empire in the eighteenth and nineteenth centuries, situating the goals of this institution in the broader expansionist wars of this period. Ruth McClure's *Coram's Children* remains a definitive work on the history of the Foundling Hospital in eighteenth-century London. Alysa Levene has reprinted several of the key texts of the Foundling Hospital in *Narratives of the Poor in Eighteenth-Century Britain* (volume 3). There are also several institutional histories by people affiliated with the Foundling Hospital: Gillian Pugh's *London's Forgotten Children* as well as John Brownlow's nineteenth-century *The History and Objects of the Foundling Hospital* are both full of details based on the authors' long affiliation with the charity. Wonderful as these resources are, they lack the direct connection with the original materials for readers that an electronic book coupled with a digitized archive can offer. Because of the embedded links to the original documents made possible through the newly digitized archive and the incredible richness of those documents, students and others interested in the Foundling Hospital now have access in ways that were previously unimaginable. My goal here is to invite readers into a discussion of the material texts themselves through a close examination of the books, papers, and forms now made available to the general reader. Until very recently this work was limited to those with access to the material records. Now this conversation can expand in the most interesting ways thanks to the digital archive.

Background of the Foundling Hospital

The Foundling Hospital addressed the seemingly intractable problem of widespread poverty by separating children from parents – usually mothers – who were presumed to be morally suspect through the simple fact of their inability to support their offspring.[2] One of the earliest institutions in England to focus specifically on infants rather than poverty more generally, the Foundling Hospital was an attempt to turn society's "unwanted" babies into respectable, hardworking laborers at the bottom of the social scale through a massive, decades-long commitment to each child admitted to the Hospital. The children were offered a limited education and modest upbringing that was designed to make them especially effective as a menial labor force, with household service for girls and farm labor or maritime service for boys.

The Hospital building was a visible (and rather grand) monument to the largess of those willing to support the reinvention of such "unwanted" babies into worthy citizens. By framing the separation of babies from their mothers at the heart of the charity into an act of generosity, the Foundling Hospital celebrated the rewards of Christian benevolence, as the site in London was both the point of separation of children from their mothers and also a site of leisure, pleasure, and even celebration for the elite benefactors who subsidized its work.

This benevolence-minded group was loosely divided among the Governors, as the refined men named to the board of the Hospital were known, and benefactors, the individuals and families whose cumulative financial donations allowed for the ongoing existence of the Hospital. Together, they were embodied in the figure of the avuncular Thomas Coram, who, while he had a complicated relationship to the institution he had founded in his lifetime, came

---

[2] Despite this presumption, the records of the Hospital seem to suggest the problem was far more about entrenched poverty, military conscription, and other circumstances than individual choices. See, for example, Alysa Levene, "The Origins of the Children of the London Foundling Hospital, 1741–1760: A Reconsideration," which points out that "a significant proportion of foundlings in this period were legitimately born" (202) while her book *Childcare, Health, and Mortality at the London Foundling Hospital 1741–1800* puts the number at 30 percent (32), as does Helen Berry (54).

Figure 1 Thomas Coram, in the foreground an infant in a basket, in the background the Foundling Hospital. Line engraving by J. Brooke, 1751, after B. Nebot, 1741.

Source: Wellcome Collection.

to represent the humane and generous intentions of this (largely) masculine space (see Figure 1).[3] While the figure of the kindly old man featured prominently in the documents and images associated with the Foundling Hospital, care in the Hospital was overseen by gentlemen in grand spaces distinct from those

---

[3] Much has been written about Thomas Coram and his relationship to the Foundling Hospital, from the effusive 1751 essay "Private Virtue and Publick Spirit Display'd ... The Character of Capt. Thomas Coram" to John Brownlow's nineteenth-century hagiography *The History and Objects of the Foundling Hospital, with a Memoir of the Founder*, 6–37. A good account of the difficulties of his final years with the Hospital is included in McClure's *Coram's Children*, 52–58.

directly involving the children, while the hands-on work was hired out to wet nurses, matrons, laundresses, maids, and cooks with little formal control over the broader processes of the Hospital.

With the reception of the first set of infants in March 1741, the institution reimagined parenthood on a completely different scale than that of a more typical British family unit.[4] The management of the children was systematized and overseen rather than valued as a set of intimate relationships, and the Governors structured parenting as a set of activities and exchanges that could be enacted through forms, committees, and financial incentives. Through the hiring out of the maternal function, the Foundling Hospital family was reinvented such that parenting was broken into a set of discrete paid tasks and child-rearing was overseen by committee. From the moment the infant arrived at the Hospital, the erasure of the biological parent(s) began; on the reception day the child was stripped of any marks of personal history or prior connection (including tokens left by parents, which were sealed away), and the institution assumed a guardianship role that was about management and training rather than nurture. Infants were sent to the countryside to be raised by a paid nurse up to about age four or five, and when the child returned to the hospital, all ties to that nurse were supposed to end. At that point a regimented, surveilled life in the institution was intended to produce a worker who could be put under apprenticeship as soon as possible (sometimes as young as age nine or ten). As well-meaning as these structures were intended to be, to the modern reader they can be astonishing in their systemic violence and casual cruelty.

Initially at the temporary Hatton Garden house and then later at the grander Foundling Hospital site in Lamb's Conduit Field in Bloomsbury, from March 1741 to June 1756, infants were admitted every few months on what was called "reception day," advertised in local papers and made known to the general public based on the financial and logistical calculations of the General Committee. Roughly twenty children usually were accepted out of the many who were presented; upon their admission, the new infants were sent off within days to be raised in the countryside for several years, until they returned as young children to the institution to be trained in menial work.[5] Through the mid

---

[4] For a more detailed history of this idea see Lawrence Stone, *The Family, Sex and Marriage in England, 1500–1800* (part 4) and Phillipe Aries, *Centuries of Childhood: A Social History of Family Life* (part 3) for a deeper history of what in the eighteenth century was a social and economic unit of parents and children with certain expectations of privacy bounded by intimate relations of love and obligation.

[5] According to McClure, the number of children admitted on any given reception day was significantly lower than the number presented for admission. See also Berry 55 and 58. Subcommittee minutes include an extensive tally of the difference between the number of children admitted from January 1749/50 to December 1755 and the number of children brought to the Hospital but turned away on each reception day (Sub-Committee Minutes, Volume 2, pages 75–76).

1750s, up to 150 children lived at the Hospital at any one time, while the much larger group of babies nursing in the country lived in individual families (McClure 76).[6] Typically between the ages of ten or twelve years old the children were apprenticed out on behalf of the Foundling Hospital and eventually "discharged" into adulthood (for boys at age twenty-four and for girls at age twenty-one or at marriage). The logistical planning for the institution was thus dizzying; infants admitted on reception days were sent within days to the countryside for up to five years (but often less) before returning either to the central London location or later to one of the several branch hospitals. Planning had to account for certain levels of mortality and was adjusted around various criteria: numbers of wet nurses available in the countryside; spaces for children as young as three or four years old in the dormitories; opportunities for apprenticeships for children as young as nine or ten years old; the possible return of children of all ages for various reasons – illness, unsuitability, and always the unexpected. Admissions thus varied significantly from year to year, and even from month to month.

This system was in place until June 1756, when the private charity received state funding from Parliament. From 1756 to 1760, the period known as the General Reception was in force. State funding mandated that all infants had to be accepted, not the carefully controlled numbers the Hospital had managed up to that point, and the age of admission was increased from under two months to up to a year.[7] Demand was staggering; admissions went from a monthly or bimonthly schedule to nearly daily, and the need was so extraordinary that satellite institutions were hastily opened (Berry 90–91, 95). Parliament became increasingly troubled by the alarming mortality statistics that emerged in the years this policy was in place; by the time Parliament withdrew funding in 1760 almost 15,000 babies had been admitted, with roughly 10,400 dying in infancy (Berry 95; McClure 102).[8]

After a period of retrenchment, in 1763, a new strategy for limiting entry was established in which mothers had to explain why they couldn't care for their children and justify what they would do instead. This significant shift in emphasis from the child to parent lasted through 1801 and marked an entirely

---

[6] Berry states, for example, that by 1756 (just before the General Reception), there were "612 children under the care of the Hospital, 189 in London, with a further 422 at nurse in the countryside" (92).

[7] For more on this period see McClure, chapters 7 and 8 in *Coram's Children*; *The Foundling Museum: An Introduction* 21–22; Berry 92–97. A sense of the magnitude of difference is captured in the Sub-Committee Minutes for October 1756, which lay out how many infants were admitted after state money was granted: rather than the 20 admitted roughly monthly before the General Reception period, in the five-day period of June 2–5 alone 195 babies were admitted (Sub-Committee Minutes, Volume 2, page 100).

[8] For more detailed statistics, see McClure, appendix 3, 261.

new approach to addressing what had been the case all along; there were simply not enough resources for the number of infants needing care.

For all its benevolent intentions, the processes established by the Foundling Hospital involved the repeated separation of children from their parents or parental figures. As Helen Berry points out, "Coram's legacy was not only to save orphans, but effectively to create them" since many (if not most) of the children given over to the Hospital's care had at least one surviving parent (Berry 277). This was certainly more convenient from the perspective of the institution, but the toll on individual lives was surely devastating, and modern accounts of former residents of the institution speak movingly of the pain of these various separations.[9] From committee minutes to billets, parental petitions to baptismal records, the archive makes visible what is said and what cannot ever be expressed and brings forward extraordinary artifacts from a defining moment in modern child-rearing practice.

My focus in the pages that follow is on the first decade and a half of this institution, from the first reception day in March 1741 to the start of the General Reception period in June 1756. This early moment set in place the philosophical principles and practices that structured the daily activities of the institution, and its records reveal both the genuine good intentions of its benefactors as well as the fundamental mismatch between their assumptions and the realities of the parents and children entering its spaces. I argue that recurring throughout these records is a striking shift toward the masculinizing of the care of infants. Over and over in the reports and forms we see a confidence in the ability of men to take over what was traditionally the nurturing work of women, with devastating effects.

The Archive

Until relatively recently the extraordinary records of this institution have largely been mined by scholars for historically specific kinds of questions: *What were the geographic and socioeconomic family origins of the foundlings? How many children were born out of wedlock in London?* Even questions quite distant from the mission of the Hospital such as *what did the clothing of everyday Britons look like?* can be answered from the voluminous and detailed records of the institution.[10] Other studies incorporate the Foundling Hospital into larger

---

[9] See, for example, Justine Cowan's account of her mother's experience in the twentieth century with the Foundling Hospital in *The Secret Life of Dorothy Soames*.

[10] See Alysa Levene's "The Origins of the Children of the Foundling Hospital, 1741–1760: A Reconsideration" for information on the foundlings in the first decade of the Hospital; Tanya Evans, *"Unfortunate Objects": Lone Mothers in Eighteenth-Century London* for information about the parents of these foundlings; Kate Gibson, "Fostering the Foundlings" on the country nurses and their relationship to the children; and John Styles, *The Dress of the People*, for details about fashions and fabrics of eighteenth-century working-class Britons.

projects, among them Donna Andrew's *Philanthropy and Police*, which examines the Foundling Hospital in the broader context of philanthropy and power in the eighteenth century and Cheryl Nixon, who focuses on the orphan both in fiction and in life in her *The Orphan in Eighteenth-Century Law and Literature*, situating the Foundling Hospital in a larger transatlantic cultural investment in parentless children.

Janette Bright and Gillian Clark have done extraordinary archival work recovering the link between individual token objects and specific billets.[11] John Ramsland, Frances Miley, and Andrew Read use the institutional history to think structurally about the affective and lived experience of foundlings and their birth parents in all kinds of ways. Some fascinating projects are in development, and the next few years promise to be quite fruitful.[12]

Indeed, what makes the entire archive so fascinating and so much more important than simply a record of a single eighteenth-century institution is the intersection of the bureaucratic impulse and the individualized archive of children's lives, or the contending forces of systematization and insistence on particularity. In that sense this archive is similar to the French police archives in the classic work of Arlette Farge, *The Allure of the Archives*, with the tension between the larger structural limits of the archive and the intensely private and personalized individual records. As such, archives speak to important ethical and logistical questions in the broader field of archive studies. The explorations of various scholars in this expansive field are instructive; in addition to challenging our notions of literacy more broadly, they offer insights into ways of reading and interpreting such often overlooked materials, as well as asking us to think more carefully about what gets preserved and from whose perspective.

Joanna Brooks's *Why We Left* offers a model for using nontraditional sources and the argument that different kinds of sources can offer fascinating insights if we approach them flexibly and with sensitivity; while her book focuses on folk ballads, it is her interpretive subtlety and her use of Indigenous studies theories to unpack such settler colonial sources that is so useful in our context. Indeed, the theoretical and structural challenges that scholars of Indigenous and African American studies have tackled have much to offer this study, where literacy and alienation from archives is such an essential part of our analysis. Saidiya

---

[11] See "The Foundling Hospital and Its Token System" (Clark and Bright) and *An Introduction to the Tokens at the Foundling Museum* (Bright and Clark). Their ongoing work is also visible on the website of the Foundling Museum: https://foundlingmuseum.org.uk/our-art-and-objects/what-youll-see.

[12] On June 23–24, 2023, The Foundling Hospital History Online Conference, sponsored by the Foundling Museum, included an array of scholars such as Kate Gibson, Claudia Soares, Claire Phillips, Beck Price, and Kristen Renzi, as well as moving conversations with former foundlings and descendants of foundlings (https://lfhconference23.wixsite.com/site/programme).

Hartman's classic *Scenes of Subjection* is a powerful reminder of the violence of the everyday as opposed to moments of extraordinary brutality. Her insights, while produced in the context of the very particular horrors of nineteenth-century American enslavement, are usefully applicable to this very different historical context. Her "Venus in Two Acts" further develops the difficulty of recovering archival traces ethically and conscientiously, as does Marisa Fuentes, *Dispossessed Lives*, which also takes on the archival traces of enslaved women in colonial archives. Tiya Miles's extraordinary and sensitive engagement with a single artifact in *All That She Carried*, in this case an embroidered sack, and its implications for our own understanding of the specificity of an experience of nineteenth-century enslavement, is a model of scholarship on what is knowable from fragmentary material artifacts. Scott Lyons's *X-Marks*, while focused on Indigenous materials and specifically treaty negotiations, homes in on the notion of the imperfect choice signaled by the "x-mark" which both signals (reluctant) assent and presence within compromised circumstances, a useful way of understanding the tokens left by anguished mothers. Finally, Kelly Wisecup's *Assembled for Use* explores alternative expressive forms that defy narrative expectation.

Most of the original buildings of the Foundling Hospital are long gone, having been demolished in the 1920s. Today that property includes a park (Coram's Fields), the home of the Coram Foundation, and the Foundling Hospital Museum, which includes salvaged elements of the original building, from a massive oak staircase to the remarkable art collection so celebrated in the eighteenth century. The remaining records of the Foundling Hospital are housed in two locations; the material objects (including a significant collection of tokens left with children) are at the Foundling Museum, which also houses an impressive archive of Handel materials. The vast majority of the documentary records for the Hospital are now in The London Archive (formerly the London Metropolitan Archive), where they have been consulted for many years by scholars and occasionally put on display. The sheer volume of these records is enormous. Covering a span of time from the early eighteenth century to the mid twentieth century, the records in The London Archive are impressive indeed, from land deeds to receipts with local vendors and tradespeople to detailed materials all associated with the London Foundling Hospital and its branch institutions. From the original parchment apprenticeship contracts of the eighteenth-century children bound out by the institution to the correspondence between interested parties to the Foundling Hospital to programs for Handel concerts in the chapel to menus for lavish fundraising meals and lists and receipts for food, clothing, and services, the physical records are extraordinary.

The records that have been digitized from the earliest period are mostly bound in leather volumes that have become increasingly fragile: committee records of the Governors of the institution as well as the billet books and general registers associated with the children that passed through the doors of the institution. There are additional records whose organization makes them more challenging to use that are divided into several other categories: the Register of Children Claimed and Petitions Claiming Children, Inspection Books for the oversight of infants in the countryside, Apprenticeship Registers, and Baptism and Burial Registers.[13] These are core records for anyone interested in the origins of the Foundling Hospital, but it is useful to remember that they represent a mere 23 percent of the total material housed at The London Archive, and many of the records related to branch hospitals are elsewhere. Even so, the production of this digital archive, with its very useful historical apparatus and easy-to-use images, is extraordinary, and it makes what was an unwieldy and dense archive available to modern readers in unprecedented ways.

The advantages of the digital archive become very clear when looking at the case of Foundling number 1102, identified by her birth mother as Mary Sly, named by the Hospital Lucy Smith. Tracing the story of this eighteenth-century child through a traditional archive would be extremely challenging. In the General Register, Volume 1 child 1102 is identified as Lucy Smith, one of the rare few who was returned to her parents, in her case her mother, on June 6, 1764, after ten years as a foundling.[14] Information pertaining to her is spread throughout the record books and is often somewhat contradictory. Her entry billet, dated June 30, 1753, includes a note that proudly identifies her as "Mary Sly, the daughter of Samuel Sly, watch Gillder, born June 29 1753" (Billet 1102, Billet Book 14), which tells us that she was one day old when she was brought to the Foundling Hospital, presumably by her mother, before being sent out to nurse. The surname her mother leaves for her is that of her father, a watch gilder, although she was instead baptized by the name Lucy Smith, one of four infants named for the Foundling Hospital by the Smith family (along with Augustus Cesar, Peter Melbury, and Nancy Monday), according to the baptismal records for July 1, 1753 (Copy Register of Baptisms and Burials). She was sent to nurse in

---

[13] The petitions included in the digital archive don't begin until 1762, outside the date range of this project. Similarly, the Register of Children forwarded from London Parishes doesn't begin until 1767 while the Nursery Books begin in the General Reception period. There are also registries from the various branch hospitals, including Ackworth, Shrewsbury, Westerham, and Chester, as well as fuller records from the Ackworth Branch Hospital, all of which invite further examination but largely fall outside the period examined here.

[14] The year 1764 was the year that the Hospital lifted its restrictive (and costly) conditions for returning children to their birth parents: Lucy Smith/Mary Sly was thus one of forty-nine children reunited with their parents in that year, the highest number of any other year for the Hospital (McClure 124).

Cowley, Middlesex until she was about five years old. The Inspection Book tells us that she was initially returned to London on July 31, 1758, although she was immediately returned to the country the same day "having a scald head" (Inspection Book, Volume 1). A year later the subcommittee minutes for July 28, 1759, instruct that she be returned from nurse in Cowley along with two other five-year-old girls "as soon as weather permits" (Subcommittee Minutes, Volume 3, pages 105–106) while the Inspection Book says she had already returned to London on July 17, 1759 (Inspection Book, Volume 1), at the age of six. The General Register suggests that the "return" was anything but smooth; she is on a list of seventeen children who were treated with the curative well water of the Powis Well at the Foundling Hospital (many for "scaled head" and eye infections) from 1759 through 1760 (Subcommittee Minutes, Volume 4, page 72). Lucy was treated for her recurring "scaled head" starting in December 1759 by drinking and washing with well water. She "was well in January relapsed in March, grew better in again in April & continues to mend."[15] In 1760, she also had smallpox as well as a bad cough (General Register, Volume 1, Child 1102). She was sent to Shrewsbury Hospital (one of the regional branches) from the main London institution in September 1762, and she appears to have lived there for two years before her mother reclaimed her (Register of Children Sent to Shrewsbury Hospital).

The Register of Children Claimed identifies her mother as Elizabeth Kent, working in 1764 as a "Housekeeper to a Gent. In Chancery Lane." Elizabeth Kent's actual petition, dated May 23, 1764, can be found in a different volume, Petitions Claiming Children, Volume 5, where she asks for her daughter by the name "Mary Sly," the name she had assigned her in the note attached to the billet ten years earlier. The child finally appears on a list of children reclaimed by their parents embedded rather curiously in the Apprenticeship Register that runs from page 301 to page 314, and then restarts on pages 329–31 (Apprenticeship Register, Volume 1, page 311). When her mother claimed her, along with her petition she reproduced the words of the note left with the one-day-old baby all those years earlier, although Samuel Sly is no longer involved in any way, as the person "giving her a very good character" is William Warren of Coleman Street and she is identified on the petition as "a spinster."

Information about the child, her parents, and her circumstances is thus dispersed throughout these records and was very difficult to piece together before digital access made much of this work more manageable. But even the relatively robust records associated with this particular child leave much that is

---

[15] The Powis Well on the grounds of the Foundling Hospital property in the 1740s was a "chalybeate spring equipped with a pumphouse, pleasure walks, and a Long Room for music and dancing" frequented by Londoners for its curative powers (McClure 62).

impossible to recover. What was her experience in the family of the nurse paid to raise her? How do we account for the different approaches to her "scaled head" and even her whereabouts at various moments? Why was she sent from London to Shrewsbury? What was it like for this child to return to her mother? How was she marked by the various transitions in her life – from Mary Sly to Lucy Smith and back again to Mary Sly, from a child raised in Middlesex to one returned to London and then moved to an institution in Shrewsbury before being taken by her mother, who was functionally a stranger to her, to a home in London? The records only offer so much, and nothing in the records can capture the child's emotional experience or even give her mother much opportunity to express herself, much less the nurse who raised her, or the inspector who oversaw her childhood, or the apothecary who treated her "scaled head."[16]

The materials contained within this archive are without question difficult to process. Our position relative to these heart-wrenching artifacts is ethically uncomfortable (these were never meant for our consumption) and emotionally difficult to process. Helen Berry, in the acknowledgments of her extraordinary study, admits to her own struggles, so familiar to anyone who has immersed themselves in these records. She writes: "When I started my research on the London Foundling Hospital archive I had no idea that it would affect me so personally or engage my emotions so directly. . . . I didn't anticipate that I would find myself caring so passionately about the foundlings whose traces I found in the voluminous bundles of documents . . . and I was afraid that I wouldn't be able to complete the project . . . in years of working with archives, I hadn't encountered anything like it" (286). We are, after all, peering at a most desperately painful moment for families at their most vulnerable. We can scrutinize objects and notes intended for a most cherished child or written in desperation by a parent whose life circumstances led to this unimaginable moment with only our own empathy to guide us. As with so many records, this is the kind of archive that no individual wants to be part of, but we have it and we should face it with respect and integrity. For Berry, this meant at a minimum refusing to repeat the demeaning serial number given to each child upon entry except in footnotes, although I have made a different decision by insisting on the very jarring juxtaposition of that number with the various names by which children were known in their lifetimes; I have tried wherever possible to honor the wishes of the birth parents by recognizing the names they assigned their infants even though these were sealed away and thus never even known by the child. Like Berry, I believe that this is not a prurient or voyeuristic exploration, but

---

[16] For different stories of reclaimed children, see Poppy Farr's blog entry on the Coram Story website, https://coramstory.org.uk/explore/content/blog/claiming-children.

rather one that honors the complexity of the situation from all sides, from the benefactors who were genuinely troubled by the suffering they encountered to the individual parents faced with life-altering decisions.

During all the phases of the eighteenth century there were distinct moments in the life of the child in relation to the institution: (1) the separation of the parent and infant on the reception day, (2) infancy in the countryside, (3) the return from the county and the indoctrination of the child into her/his laboring life at the Hospital, and (4) apprenticeship under the auspices of the Hospital. At core, however, there was one essential divide: the days or weeks of the child's life before the Foundling Hospital, and then the life structured around its rules and systems. Each is documented in the records of the Hospital and attached to a particular account or set of documents for each stage in the process of producing the infant as a useful citizen. The sheer number of infants, nearly 1,400, who passed through the doors of the Foundling Hospital in the first phase of its existence even as the buildings were built and the infrastructures were established meant that the benevolent function of the institution was strained to its very limits.

The sections that follow move roughly chronologically through the phases of a foundling's relationship to the Hospital in the first fifteen years of the institution, juxtaposing published texts like *An Account of the Hospital for the Maintenance and Education of Exposed and Deserted Young Children* (1749) and *An Essay upon Nursing* (1748), written by physician William Cadogan for the Foundling Hospital, with the actual records of the Hospital newly made available through the digital archive.[17] In Section 1, I focus on the reception day, the day infants were surrendered to the institution, usually by their birth parent(s). In particular, I examine the tension between the details of the reception day from the perspective of the Governors of the institution and the two moments in the archive in which birth parents (mostly mothers) are visible: the information recorded on the Hospital's entry billet and the tokens left by those mothers as a potential avenue to retrieving their children should their circumstances change. By combing through these records and cross-referencing other materials in the archive I argue for a much more nuanced perspective on what the institution presented as a benevolent and humane process.

Section 2 focuses on the foundling experience, from the fostering system through which infants were raised outside of London for several years under

---

[17] I cite these throughout from two sources (unless otherwise specified): as originally paginated in the 1749 edition of *An Account of the Hospital for the Maintenance and Education of Exposed and Deserted Young Children* and also as reprinted in Alysa Levene's *Narratives of the Poor* (Volume 3), a volume devoted exclusively to texts related to the Foundling Hospital in the eighteenth century. My references to *An Essay upon Nursing*, William Cadogan, include pagination from the original (anonymous) 1748 version and as it is reprinted in Levene's collection.

the supervision of the Foundling Hospital to the apprenticeship that usually characterized the last years of a child's relationship to the Hospital. In the first part I argue that Cadogan's text on nursing is emblematic of the larger trend at the Foundling Hospital of replacing women's maternal labor with male authority and structures of expertise and power, while the lived experiences of children and their dependence on women's labor suggest a far more complicated dynamic. The return of young children to the institution, typically when children were about four or five years old until they reached the age of ten or twelve, when they were generally apprenticed out until adulthood, was a period of indoctrination and training for menial jobs. By focusing on sources as varied as hymns sung by the children, apprentice instructions, and descriptions of the physical space, I explore the ways children's experience of benevolence within the gates of the London institution was often an exercise in humility and lowered expectations. In the conclusion, I lay out some of the complexities of the way benevolent intentions confronted the lived experience of the children through the tangible marks of the historical archive. Connecting the General Register with its carefully enumerated list of children in order of entry into the Hospital to the Apprenticeship Register, with its organizational challenges in recording the experiences of children as they moved into this final phase of their relationship to the institution, the orderly succession the Hospital envisioned collapses and the complexity of individuals lives lived and reordered and reframed emerges throughout the lines of these pages.

1 Reception Day

Preparations

Planning for the first reception day, the day needy infants would be separated from their birth families and taken into the institution, took years. The first set of children was received into the Foundling Hospital on March 25, 1741, but long before that there was the work of petitioning and fundraising for the kind of institution that would take in abandoned babies. That extended process culminated in a ladies' petition (1729) that lamented "the frequent Murders committed on poor miserable Infants by their Parents, to hide their Shame, and the inhuman Custom of exposing new-born Children to perish in the Streets, or training them up in Idleness, Beggary, and Theft" (*An Account* 3–4; Levene 19) and galvanized its elite members into action to protect these children. This petition by "Ladies of Quality and Distinction" (*An Account* iii; Levene 8) seemed to promise that women not only acceded to an arrangement through which men institutionalized and dominated child-rearing by removing children from their mothers, but actively sought it out, further cementing the complicated class and gender fault lines of the institution. A decade later, in

1739, a Royal Charter was established for the institution to begin its work in earnest. Then came the seemingly endless discussions of logistics, which are visible in a more unvarnished form in the administrative committee records (General Court Rough Minutes, Volumes 1 and 2; Daily Committee Minutes and House Committee Minutes, and Sub-Committee Minutes, Volumes 1 and 2). The General Court Rough Minutes begin November 20, 1739, formally incorporating the charity under the charter. These minutes summarize what were surely boisterous meetings of the gentlemen founders held at "Mr Manaton's great Room in the Strand," otherwise known as The Crown and Anchor Tavern (Compston 100). For a year and a half, they established the ground rules, set up the logistics, found the property, and organized structures for accepting financial donations and managing children. There were comparisons with continental institutions, reports of committees and subcommittees, and arguments over wording, strategies, finances, and logistics. These were giddy, abstracted conversations among men genuinely touched by the fate of the poor children of London. In October 1740, the first draft of the rules by which children were to be accepted was entered into the record (General Court Rough Minutes, Volume 1), with specific line edits noted.[18] In that same month, the group also authorized the purchase of the land upon which the Hospital was to be built (General Court Rough Minutes, Volume 1).

The sense of urgency of the original members of the board was tempered by the dizzying logistical challenges. Temporary quarters in Hatton Garden were taken as the grander hospital was being built, and the Daily Committee Minutes and House Committee Minutes, starting in 1740 and running well into 1742, delve into the finer points of running the institution: the hiring of staff, purchasing of clothing, and organizing admissions, as well as discussions of how to manage and identify individual babies in the earliest years of the institution. These records document the extraordinary effort that went into Hospital operations; it was far from an abstracted exercise. The Governors were involved in the minutia of children's care, from selecting clothes to troubleshooting everything from children's' illnesses (and death) to the logistics of travel to Yorkshire (among other places) for infants and their nurses. While men were making the decisions, the Hospital clearly operated through the work of women, from "Ladies of Fashion" to nurses and housemaids and other servants who variously advised, cooked or cleaned, and tended the children. These appear throughout the notes and deliberations of the committee. The Daily Committee Minutes for the first year show both an extraordinary commitment to children's welfare and a surprisingly nimble ability to shift practices as situations called for it to

---

[18] This was published as *A Sketch of the General Plan for Executing the Purposes of the Royal Charter* along with *The Report of the General Committee* in 1740, before a single child had been admitted to the Hospital.

a nearly overwhelming sense of chaos barely mitigated, from managing the theft of clothing (Daily Committee Minutes and House Committee Minutes, page 17) to the perpetual hiring and dismissing of nurses. Even as they were managing the daily care of children, the Governors were equally preoccupied with setting precedents in terms of the information gathered on various forms and the kinds of books and records to be maintained (see, for example, Daily Committee Minutes and House Committee Minutes, page 31 and Daily Committee Minutes and House Committee Minutes, page 33).

The Governors were eager to make their work visible to the general public, starting with the publication of their initial plans in 1740 and including regular updates in local newspapers. However *An Account of the Hospital for the Maintenance and Education of Exposed and Deserted Young Children*, first printed in 1749, eight years after the first set of children was admitted, was the clearest public-facing document representing the Foundling Hospital.[19] An astonishing text, simultaneously idealistic and deeply practical, it captures the planning and organizing rather than the experience of the children, and its emphasis is on replicable systems rather than individual stories. This is the Hospital as it should be in the minds of its Governors: a permanent, highly regularized institution with clear rules and guidelines for everything from accepting donations to annual meetings to raising children. Perhaps unsurprisingly, *An Account* maintains a sense of general well-being and the idealism of good intentions rather than focusing on the anguish of separation and loss. *An Account* establishes bureaucracies and structures of pain mitigation by focusing on benefactors rather than children, systems rather than individual experiences.

According to *An Account*, the goal of the Foundling Hospital, one celebrated by the respectable women who signed the early ladies' petition as well as all the benefactors involved in its inception, was to turn children from the destructive path their birth parents had them on and lead those children instead toward becoming "useful Members of the Common-Wealth" (*An Account* iv; Levene 8). More specifically, the institution was "for the better producing good and faithful Servants from amongst the poor and miserable cast-off Children or Foundlings, now a Pest to the Publick and a chargeable Nuisance within the Bills of Mortality" (*An Account* iv; Levene 8–9). The stark divide between the benefactors (the Hospital) and those needing its largesse (children and their "failed" parents) is clear, and the relationship between the needs of the two groups (good servants for the benefactors, steady employment for "cast-off Children") is made explicit.

---

[19] This text appears in multiple editions throughout the eighteenth century, which expand and alter the rules and structures of the Hospital as applicable. In addition to a brief historical overview, this text includes the ladies' petition, charter, act of incorporation, and bylaws of the Hospital.

Written from the perspective of benefactors and with minute attention to their concerns, *An Account* describes the public spaces of the Hospital in great detail, while there is only passing mention of the children's accommodations. We are told that "soon after the Hospital became habitable, several eminent Masters of Painting, Sculpture, and other Arts, were pleased to contribute many elegant Ornaments, which are placed in the Hospital, as Monuments of their Charity, and Abilities in their several Arts" (*An Account* xiii–xiv; Levene 14). The grand rooms of the first floor were ornate public spaces, with an impressive art collection and formal meeting rooms for the Governors who oversaw all elements of the Foundling Hospital's existence, from its finances to the details of childcare. The extensive grounds contained a large park open to the public, a popular site for strolling and entertainment where the children's labors were put on display (see Figure 2). The chapel too was a fine and ornate space, where the elegant people of London came to observe the children and involve themselves in the broader spirit of benevolence that the Hospital celebrated.[20]

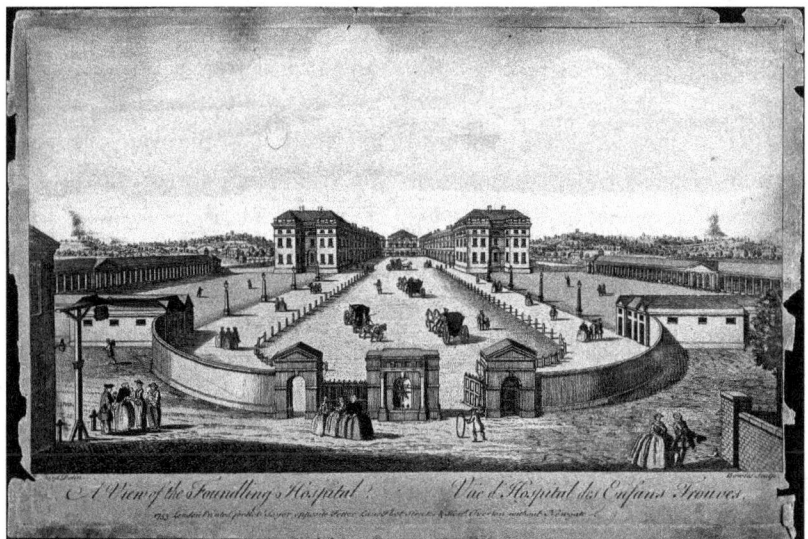

Figure 2 The Foundling Hospital, Holborn, London: a bird's-eye view of the courtyard. Colored engraving by T. Bowles after L. P. Boitard, 1753. Public Domain Mark.

Source: Wellcome Collection.

---

[20] See Berry 70–76 for more information about the art gallery and ornate touches of the public rooms; see also pages 546–54 of Michael Cohen's article "Addison, Blake, Coram, and the London Foundling Hospital" on philanthropy and art in the Foundling Hospital collections, especially the relationship between Coram and Hogarth. See also McClure 65–72.

As a public-facing document, through an emphasis on financial and logistical information, *An Account* occludes the anguish of the separation of parent and child that is at the heart of the institution. In this telling, infants and children are subsumed to "Premises" and "Accounts" of the Hospital (*An Account* 9; Levene 23). Those accounts, carefully examined, audited, and made public, are evidence of compassion, and can even be said to replace infant bodies as evidence of care. These records emphasize the interests and investments of the benefactors: "All Persons who shall subscribe and pay to the said Corporation to the Amount of Twenty Pounds, or more, or of Forty Shillings or more, annually, shall have free Liberty to inspect the said Hospital, and inform themselves of the State thereof, and of the manner of nursing, dieting, managing, instructing and employing the Children therein" (*An Account* 10–11; Levene 23). Whether inspecting the books or scrutinizing the children and their care, all aspects of the Hospital were available to benefactors (for a fee). The business of the Foundling Hospital was thus presented as efficiently transactional, and its meticulous documentation and accounting gave meaning to the suffering at its core.

This intertwining of benevolence and suffering was especially visible in the case of what is without a doubt the most emotionally fraught moment orchestrated by the Hospital: the reception day through which women and their babies were parted. The admissions procedures detailed in *An Account* are startling both in their precision and in their abstraction. While these procedures certainly shifted over time (the lottery system, for example, was instituted after the first few chaotic reception days as a strategy of crowd control), their general form seems to have stayed in place at least until the population explosion of the General Reception period after 1756. On the reception day, everything was accounted for. The porter opened the gate at a specific time to anyone who brought a child (not more than one child at a time) and nobody else was allowed in except Governors and "such as they give Orders to be admitted" (*An Account* 56; Levene 52).[21] Then "the Persons, who bring Children, are . . . conducted into a large Room, and ordered to seat themselves on Benches; those who bring Boys at one End of the Room, and those who bring Girls at the other, and not to leave their Places, till called" (*An Account* 56–57; Levene 52). Once the posted time has passed, the account continues, "a Bell is to be rung, the Doors of the Hospital are to be shut, and no Person admitted to bring a Child after that

---

[21] Exceptions were made for at least two sets of twins who were admitted in the first decade of the hospital (child 373 [Billet 373, Billet Book 5] and child 377 [Billet 377, Billet Book 5], and child 513 [Billet 513, Billet Book 6] and child 520 [Billet 520, Billet Book 6]). Neither set of twins was marked as related in the names they were assigned in the General Register (General Register, Volume 1, Child 373 and Child 377) and (General Register, Volume 1, Child 513 and Child 520). See also McClure, 142.

Time" (*An Account* 57; Levene 52). Two of the Governors then counted the number of children there and prepared the marble-sized balls for the lottery. For every twenty white balls there were four red balls, and then as many black balls as to account for all the babies in the room; this was done separately for the boys and for the girls. The purpose of this life-altering lottery was to determine which children among the many brought on the reception day were to be admitted.

An Account quietly acknowledges that for all the brisk efficiency of the processes outlined in its pages, the vast majority of people bringing infants were mothers who were at best ambivalent about leaving their babies: "Each Person who shall draw a Black Ball, shall immediately be led by the Messenger, with *her* Child, out of the Hospital" (*An Account* 57; Levene 52; italics mine).[22] The account continues: the person selecting a white ball "is to be carried into a Room alone, there to remain, till such a Time as *her* Child shall be received, or refused" (*An Account* 58; Levene 53; italics mine). The child was taken to yet another room, where she/he was undressed in the presence of the matron, "and if the Physician, Surgeon, or Apothecary, attending, shall have any Suspicion of its having any infectious Distemper; or if it appears to be above the Age of two Months, it shall be returned to the Person who brought it, in the Cloaths in which it was brought, and shall be taken immediately out of the Hospital." On the other hand, "If there is no such Objection, it is to be received, and the Person who brought it dismissed" (*An Account* 58; Levene 53). There is a brisk efficiency to the movement of the infant into one space and the parental figure into another, with periods of waiting and examination described in the most neutral language. However, the pronoun references reveal what the account tries to diminish; the infant is referred to as "it," while the neutral-sounding "parent" is acknowledged as a "her," a mother facing a piercingly difficult decision whose outcome is miserable either way. There was no room for final farewells or second thoughts, just a flurry of uncertainty until "the Person" (the mother) was "dismissed" without seeing her child again.

The extent of the suffering in this moment – both for those whose children are accepted and those who are turned away – is masked in logistical detail. However, the pain is captured in the unpublished minutes of the General

---

[22] There are certainly exceptions. It is not always the mother leaving the baby, as several notes indicate. For example, in March 1741, infant number 21 (Billet 21, Billet Book 1), a two-month-old boy, was left with a note saying "Child is not Christned – The Father not found – The Mother has Deserted it Mothers name is Dorothy Smith March 25th 1741." The facts make clear that neither the mother nor the father are with the child. Another note left with a month-old girl (child 676) inexpertly explains: "Born november 6 1750 is o bliged reather then peeash to be left to the charedy of the generus Benefacters of the fundeling house by the unhappy death of its father and the mothers lifes being despaird of from Gentlemen and ladys with prayse till death for you all" (Billet 676, Billet Book 8). In addition, several notes make clear that the mother and the father make the decision jointly.

Committee in the extended description of the first reception day in March 1741 (Daily Committee Minutes and House Committee Minutes, page 6 and Daily Committee Minutes and House Committee Minutes, page 7). These soberingly report that "the Expressions of Grief of the Women whose Children could not be admitted were Scarcely more observable than those of some of the Women who parted with their Children, so that a more moving Scene can't well be imagined" (also quoted in McClure 50). For all the logistical order and efficiency that *An Account* promises, the actual scene on reception days must have been chaotic, loud, and frantic. Notably, that fraught moment with its abrupt and uncertain separations is cited as "a moving scene" whose effect on observers (benefactors) is more important than what is experienced by the actual parent(s) and child undergoing separation. This is reinforced in the description of the day after the children are received, when "many Charitable Persons of Fassion [Fashion] visited the Hospital, and whatever share Curiosity might have in inducing any of them to Come, none went away without shewing most Sensible marks of Compassion for the helpless objects of this Charity and few /if any/ without contributing something for their Relief" (Daily Committee Minutes and House Committee Minutes, page 8).

At this point, the child is considered fully the responsibility of the Hospital, and the strategies for both marking and erasing her/his identity come into tension. *An Account* explains: "Every Child received is to have a different Letter of the Alphabet tied to its Wrist." The letter on the tag attached to child's wrist is matched to her/his assigned wet nurse, who has the same letter pinned to her sleeve. This letter connecting the infant to her/his assigned wet nurse is recorded on the billet, the form that documents the entry of each admitted child (see Figure 3). After noting the letter, the billet identifies "the Sex and supposed Age of the Child, the Year and Day when inspected, the Particulars of the Child's Dress, the Marks, if any on its Body; and particular Mention is to be made, in such Billet, of any Writing, or other Thing, brought with the Child." (*An Account* 58; Levene 53). In the march toward institutional life, the letter tag and the "Writing, or other Thing" are transitional, a brief acknowledgment of the infant's life before the Foundling Hospital carefully documented on the institutional form called the billet.

The letter(s), both the tag by which the child is assigned to a wet nurse and also the "Writing or other Thing" of the parent, pull in both directions; they connect the child to her/his birth parent(s) and to the wet nurse who will care for the child for the next few years. However the letter is temporary since it is exchanged for a number the following day. For the rest of her/his time at the institution, the child is identified with a number stamped onto a metal tag permanently associated with the Hospital, unlike the transitory letter(s).

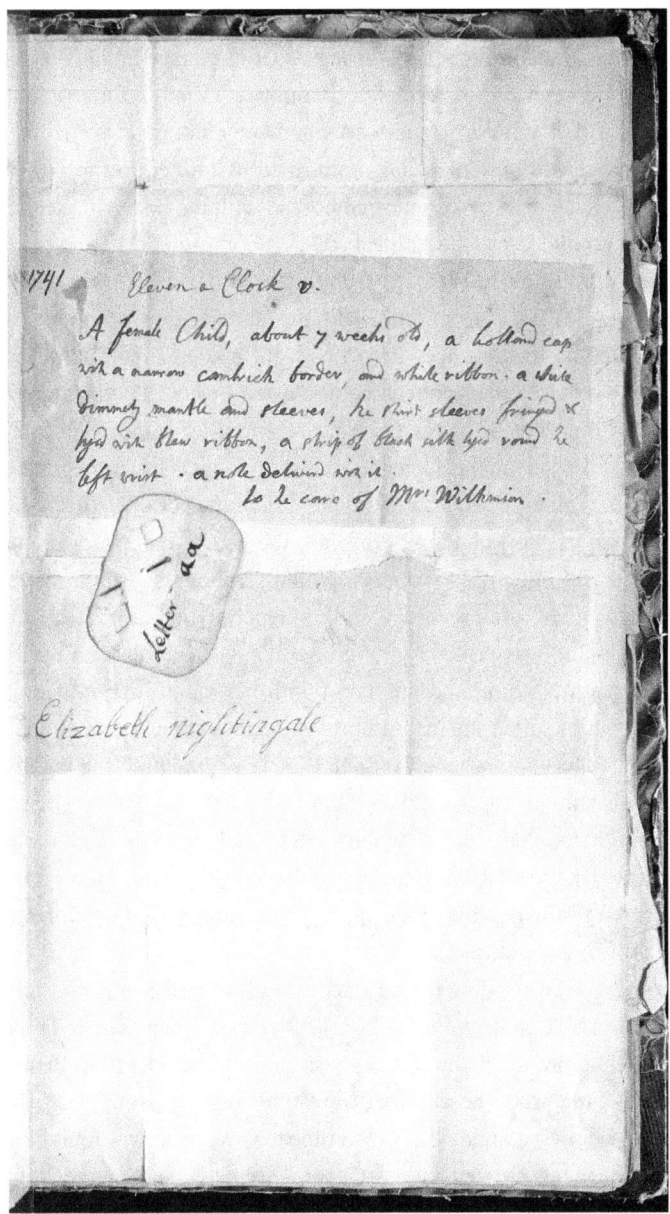

Figure 3 A sample billet with a letter tag [A-FH-A-09-001-001-089]. Notice that the leather tag ("letter aa") is pinned to the parental note, which is the child's original name ("Elizabeth Nightingale"); both are attached to the early billet, which is in the form of a brief description of the infant's clothes and the time of admission.

Source: Coram Foundation.

An Account is adamant that "Great Care is to be taken, that the Number always remains fixed to the Child, during its Continuance in the Hospital" (*An Account* 61; Levene 55). The Daily Committee minutes for the first set of children are filled with references to numbers coming loose from babies' necks and having to be replaced or confirmed as affixed to the proper child, leading to the system of pewter tags embossed with the hospital's seal attached with ribbon around each child's neck (Daily Committee Minutes and House Committee Minutes, page 17; Daily Committee Minutes and House Committee Minutes, page 18; Daily Committee Minutes and House Committee Minutes, page 25). Even so those tags came off as well, much to the frustration of the Governors, who were very concerned about the proper identification of each child (Daily Committee Minutes and House Committee Minutes, page 29). This number was marked in the General Register, logged in the Apprenticeship Register, and in all cases was the permanent identifier of the child.

By the logic of the Foundling Hospital, the process stripped infants of all previous parental influences – names, clothes, mementos – and moved them toward a new identity as recorded in the General Register. Each infant was reinvented; she/he was remade through her/his association with the hospital, marked (through clothing and numbers) with her/his affiliation and assigned a value that better suited the institution. When all went as planned, the mother returned to her life with a receipt (after 1759) documenting the details of her child's admission to the Hospital;[23] the wet nurse and the numbered and renamed child also departed a few days later, while the billet and the parental letter remained in the Hospital at the end of the reception day. Each was properly matched through the deployment of tags, forms, and sealed documents, as *An Account* confidently outlines.

While the administration of the institution required a number for proper documentation and control, the child also received a new name. The number was assigned before the name and severed the birth parents from their child in the Hospital's records. The children were typically received on a Friday and baptized the following Sunday, at which time they were given a foundling name, and that name was marked in the General Register and in the Register of Baptisms, regardless of the child's previous baptismal status and any instructions left by parents about names. Naming in this case was a financially lucrative moment for the Hospital: "The Names are to be given to the Children, by the Governors, and other charitable Persons present, at which Time, the Charity of the Persons Present, shall be collected" (*An Account* 62; Levene 55).

---

[23] The receipts, instituted in 1759, identified the gender of the child and the date of the admission, and were signed by the receiving clerk. See Clark and Bright 54.

Donors and benefactors were granted naming privileges as part of the broader transition of the infant to a foundling. The Register of Baptisms shows the evolution of this practice. The first attempt at recordkeeping documents the child's number, the page upon which the child appears in the General Register, and the name of the minister performing the baptism. This is revised a few pages later to deemphasize the name of the minister and include the name of the benefactor selecting the name, highlighting the importance of the donor rather than the minister (Copy Register of Baptisms, Volume 1). The first few children were named directly for their benefactors: Thomas Coram names his selected infant Thomas Coram, Sarah Richmond is named by the Duchess of Richmond, and so on. The subcommittee records indicate that in the first group of babies the boys were named by the (male) Governors, and the girls were named by "Ladies of Fashion" (Sub-Committee Records, Volume 1, page 9). There seems to be a delight in these early days in claiming a child in a very particular way by bestowing the benefactor's name upon the infant – a kind of merging of ownership and benevolence.

This convention didn't last long; practically speaking, benefactors who named more than one child couldn't sustain it, and it seems that the younger members of the benefactor cohort (the "Misses" identified on the register) were the earliest to break with this. On May 10, 1741, Miss Lucretia Folkes named foundling number 80 Ethelred Hovell in a grandiose gesture toward Saxon royalty (having earlier named a baby after herself) while Miss Wilhelmina Manley named foundling number 89 Pamela Andrews, a nod toward a popular fictional character (Copy Register of Baptisms, Volume 1). Names thus shifted from being self-referential to becoming more fanciful, folding infants into the imaginative and cultural context of their upper-class patrons. While some benefactors continued to name infants after themselves, we also find more fanciful names such as James Cape Breton, East Street, and Ethelred Grantham (Copy Register of Baptisms, Volume 1); Geoffrey Chaucer and William Shakespear both were admitted to the Hospital in 1751 (General Register, Volume 1, Child 684 and Child 709).

Relationships were invented through the vagaries of benefactor naming practices: Bennet Bishop and Thomas Bishop, foundlings 69 and 70 respectively, were both named by a Mrs. Colt with the same last name, suggesting a sibling relationship (Copy Register of Baptisms, Volume 1). However their billets indicate that other than entering the Foundling Hospital on the same night they had nothing in common; foundling 69 was a two-month-old girl named by her parent Ann Coffee, while foundling number 70 was a six-week-old boy also left with a note (Billet 69, Billet Book 1 and Billet 70, Billet Book 1). The first child was sent to Nurse Webb while the second went with Nurse Davis. The first died within weeks of entering the Hospital while the second was apprenticed out in 1753 (General Register, Volume 1, Child 69 and Child 70). Naming offered benefactors (especially women benefactors) an opportunity to memorialize their contributions, but it also marked a curious sort of abstraction. Despite being named after a benefactor, infants were then whisked away for years at a time, and whatever influence benefactors may have intended to have, they were largely absent from the child's life after that one baptismal moment. Rather than establishing a connection, benefactor naming practices severed babies from their earlier lives without establishing any other lasting commitments between specific babies and the benefactors they were named by and for.

Billets

Broadly speaking, the billet was the crucial conduit between the infant brought to the Hospital with one name, set of clothes, and relations at the time of reception and the number and alternative name and identity by which she/he was known institutionally in the General Register. The form through which an infant was initially documented for the Hospital, the billet is a curiously weighted document, a container of identity and a marker of difference, albeit an unstable one in a moment of transition defined by letter tags, shifting names, and movement from room to room, from parent to matron to nurse. The General Register, a set of enormous bound volumes listing ten children per page, defined foundling life. The Register lists the Hospital's information about each of the thousands of children received into the Foundling Hospital in the eighteenth century stripped of all reference to their origins: the child's new name, number, health record going forward, and assignments such as the child's nurse, apprentice, etcetera (see Figure 4). The billet, on the other hand, marked the past life – the clothes the child wore before the uniform, the original name of the child (if indicated in a note), and on occasion evidence of love and loss left by a desperate parent. These two sets of records were kept separately, and unless a parent returned for a child (few ever did) the billet was to remain sealed forever.

Filled out for each infant by Hospital agents, the billet was an uneasy conduit between the child, the parent, and the hospital. While the initial billets were simply blank pieces of paper filled out individually (Figure 3), they were quickly (within the first year) produced as a standardized printed form (Figure 5). The information collected for each child remained roughly the same throughout the eighteenth century: gender, age, time of entry, and a brief description of the body and/or clothing of the child. *An Account* explains the central function of the billets: "These Billets being the only Means, which

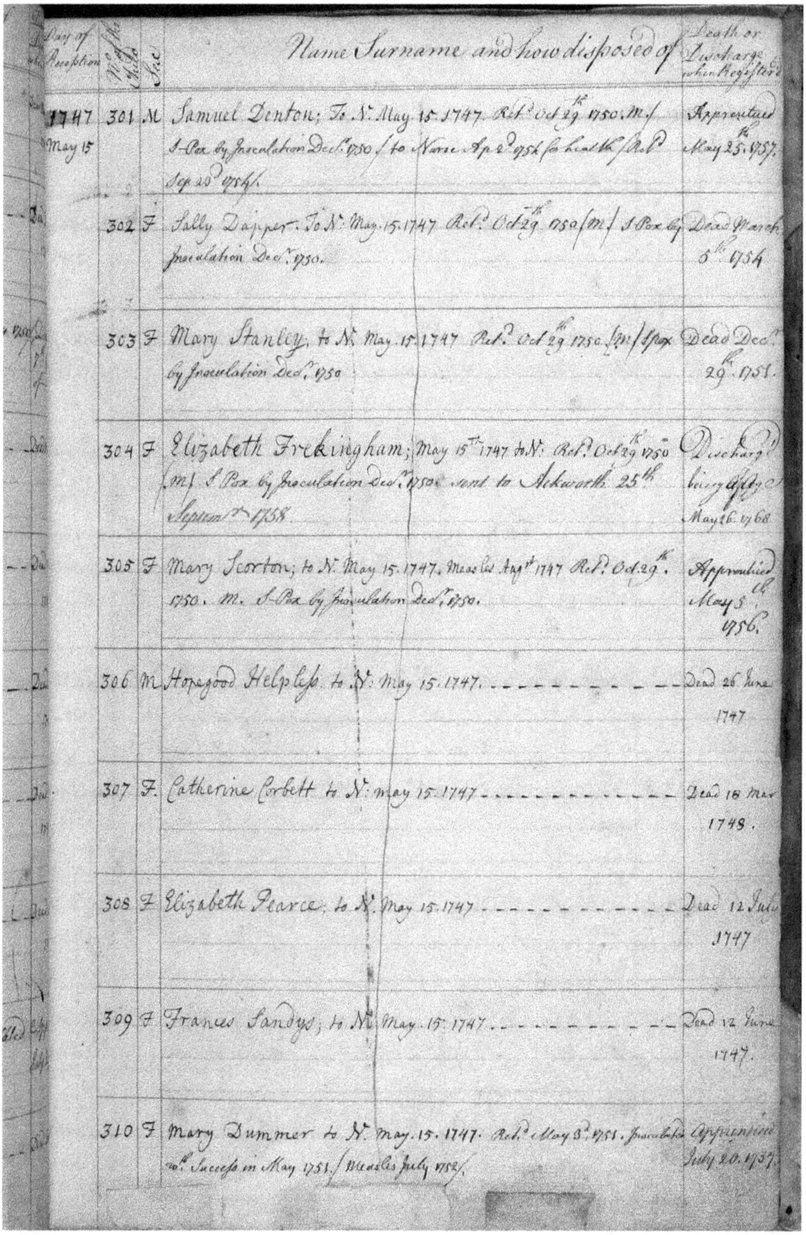

Figure 4 A page from the General Register, Volume 1 [A-FH-A-09-002-001-037]. Ten children are listed on each page, with columns for each child's number, gender, foundling name, any actions such as inoculations or other treatments, and final outcomes ("Death or Discharge," or possibly apprentice date).

Source: Coram Foundation.

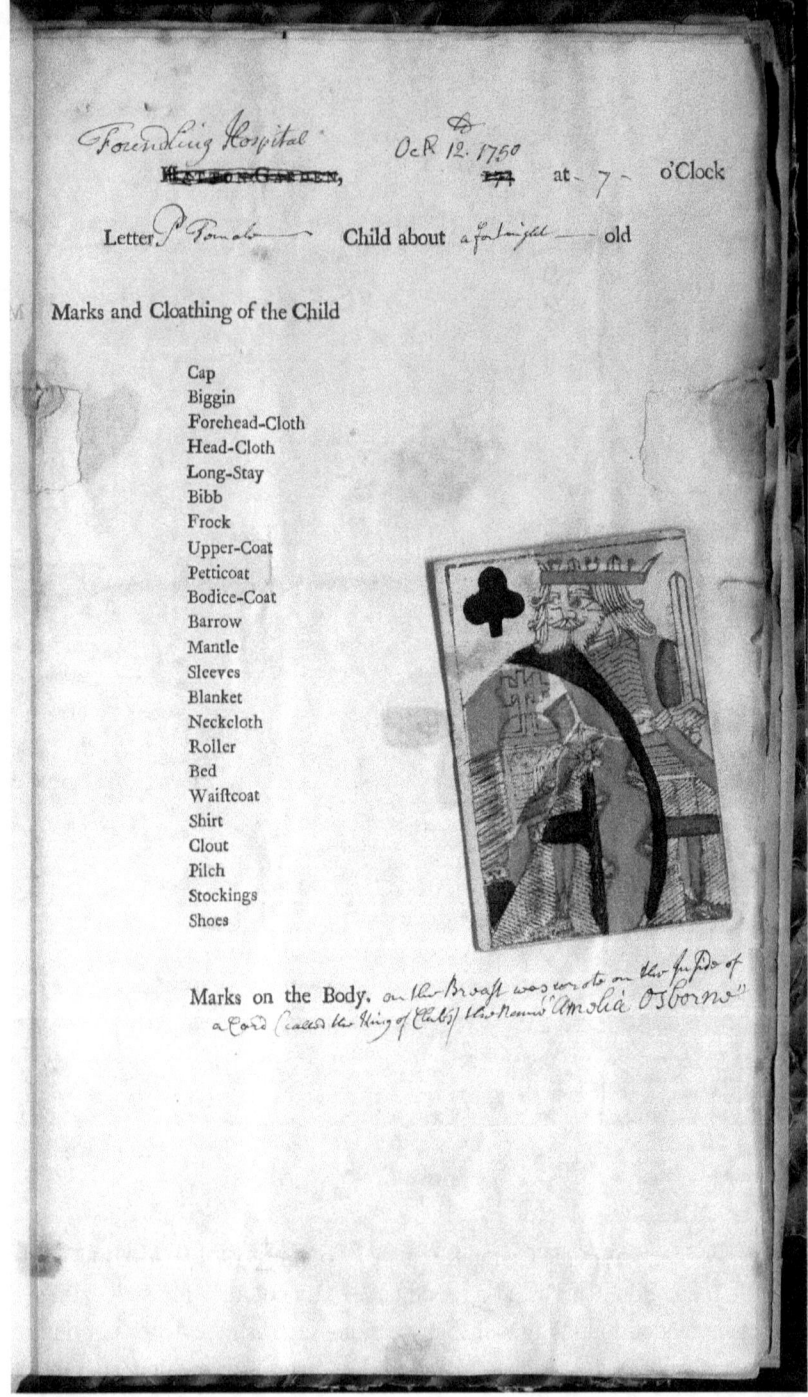

Figure 5 A sample billet with pinned token [A-FH-A-09-001-008-113]. The token (in this case a playing card inscribed on the back with the child's name,

can inable the Governors to know the Children, in Case they should be inquired for at any future Time, are to be kept with great Care and Secrecy, in a secure Place provided for that Purpose" (*An Account* 62; Levene 55).[24] Billets were sealed away, removed from the rest of the forms and structures the Hospital maintained about its foundlings. They ostensibly existed to facilitate the possible reunion of birth parent and child, but only at the pleasure of the Hospital. These forms are in service to the mission of the Hospital rather than an aide for parents, who are rhetorically erased from the transaction in this description through the strategic use of the passive voice. Parents get access to their own children at the will of the Governors, and only Governors can "know" children while parents cannot. The secrecy with which billets were treated suggested a kind of quarantine; in their sealed-off state, the billets were potential contaminants for the impressionable children of the Foundling Hospital, to be unsealed only in extraordinary circumstances carefully monitored by the Governors.

However, scholar Maria Zytaruk characterizes the billet very differently: "Because each billet served as a receptacle for whatever items arrived with the child (notes, verses, textiles, objects), these documents are properly understood as miniature, self-contained archives" ("Unruly Objects" 41). Carefully filled out, sealed, and kept together with the other billets from the same day in a process that was minutely managed, as we have seen, each billet marked the ways individual children were distinct from each other. The secrecy that surrounded each billet was predicated on the assumption that the children these forms represented were unwanted, and that parents were desperate to return to their lives without the burden of a child. They could do so, according to the logic of the Foundling Hospital, only by severing all ties to their children, a process that was assured through rigorous protections of secrecy. However, as Zytaruk's characterization makes clear, the billets also functioned as a carefully preserved archive of the life before with an insistence on the possibility of

---

Caption for Figure 5 (cont.)

Amelia Osborne) replaces any description of the clothes for child 656, although the top is filled in with the date and time of reception ("Oct 12th 1750 at 7 o'Clock"), letter assigned to the child ("P"), the gender ("Female"), and approximate age of the child ("a fortnight old").

Source: Coram Foundation.

---

[24] Of the 11,037 children brought into the hospital through 1758, only 44 were returned to their parents, according to the 1758 edition of *An Account*. See Clark and Bright 58–60 for a more detailed discussion of the records connected to claimed children.

reunification. In this sense the billet marked not the parents' desire to forget their child, but rather often detailed instructions on how to be remembered. The tokens left with the children as well as the information on the billets seem to suggest something very different from the Hospital's assumptions; far from desiring secrecy, many parents not only seemed to want their children to know them but also very much wanted to know what happened to their children. Over and over we see parents documenting precisely the kind of information the Hospital sought to hide: the name of the mother and/or father, for example, or specific information about the child's place of origin or moment of birth.

Whatever wishes the parent(s) may have expressed, the effect of the mandated erasure of the life before was that once they were separated from their clothing and other tokens, the children were interchangeable from the perspective of the Hospital. Certainly the information collected on the billets suggests that the children were indistinguishable without a prepared tag or number; other than the occasional notice of a particular physical feature (misshapen limbs, moles, warts, and birthmarks) very little separated one child from another, especially since before the General Reception period, the upper age limit for admission was a mere two months. The billet thus sealed all evidence of distinctiveness away, producing the infant as an object to be dressed and numbered according to the rules of the institution. However, even as they suggested order and control, the billets also revealed the possibility of loss, confusion, and exchange. For example, the note at the bottom of the billet for baby 374 indicates, "The Porter Says this is the Child mentioned in that Letter delivered sometime herein by me[?] to Mr White & has after here before the Committee – that Letter the Porter seems taken notice of this Childs [illeg Lox?] but he has forgot – whether it is a Boy or Girl," leaving in question if the note identifying the baby as Elizabeth Wall, daughter of Mary Wall, is attached to the right child (Billet 374, Billet Book 5). Similarly, child 376 has a series of notations on her billet: "Memorandum The Child has on a Red and white flowerd new Gown and a white Ribbon about her head and is Babtized by a Church minister by the name of Jane Gilbert." Below on the note but in a different hand: "This was bro't to the Hospital on the 20th of Der 1747 wch was Sayed by the person who bid it to belong to one of the Children brot in Last Friday Evening Expects soon to take it out again." However, under "Marks on the Body," the following note is written: "no such Gown was brought to the Hospitall nor is there any other mark or description to ascertain this Child to belong to the paper enclosed Except that no other child brought this Night has any white Ribbon on except 2 both which had papers delivered with the Children" (Billet 376, Billet Book 5). In each of these situations, the assurance of the system of lettering and numbering comes into question, and the billet, the cornerstone of the transitional paperwork, only imperfectly marks the identity of any individual child (Billet 368, Billet Book 5).

In fact, the institution was often at a loss as to how to differentiate these children. There is certainly a sense on the initial billets that identifying children is no easy business; some show a careful study of infant bodies such as this one for child 24: "March 25.1741 A female child 3 weeks old with . . . a mole between the shoulders and a mark on the inside of the right arm" (Billet 24, Billet Book 1), or child 51, who is "very poorly drest" and also has "a red [mark?] under the left breast" (Billet 51, Billet Book 1). Some of the early billets have an extensive detailing of clothes and objects left with the child that might be meaningful, while others simply say something like "A female child about a month old without any mark" (Billet 12, Billet Book 1), or "A Male child about 6 weeks old. no mark" (Billet 15, Billet Book 1). In these cases, it is unclear if the bodies are unmarked, or if there are no tokens left with the children. Either way, the child has only the most general identifiers: gender and a rough estimate of age.

The billets mark the initial impressions of the caretakers of the institution, many of which are almost exclusively about the children's clothes. These observations reveal a range of class assumptions. A sampling from the first year suggests the metric that continued throughout the admissions billets of the first decade: "Meanly dressed" (Billet 68, Billet Book 1); "cleanly drest" (Billet 66, Billet Book 1); "very neatly dressed" (Billet 31, Billet Book 1); "very ragged and meanly dressed" (Billet 36, Billet Book 1); "extremely clean and neat" (Billet 53, Billet Book 1); or simply "neat" (Billet 74, Billet Book 1) or "mean" (Billet 71, Billet Book 1). More rarely, signs of clear bodily distress were noted: "seemed stupefied with opium" (Billet 37, Billet Book 1); "almost starved" (Billet 11, Billet Book 1); "very weakly" (Billet 26, Billet Book 1). That is, whatever clothes the child came in would be removed, and whatever state the (damaged) body was in could be fixed; a starving child could be fed, a drugged child could be taken off of drugs, and a weak body could be strengthened. In all cases, the infant was a blank slate to be remade by the institution.

The information collected for each child was more regularized once the printed billet form was put into place, although this form was contingent on the person filling it out. Each form listed the letter, date, time of entry, age, and gender of the child. And just as the handwritten papers that predated the form focused mainly on clothing, the bulk of the space on the printed page is taken up with the list of potential items of clothing titled "Marks and Cloathing of the Child." That list is extensive: "Cap, Biggin, Forehead Cloth, Head-Cloth, Long-Stay, Bibb, Frock, Upper-Coat, Petticoat, Bodice-Coat, Barrow, Mantle, Sleeves, Blanket, Neckcloth, Roller, Bed, Waistcoat, Shirt, Clout, Pilch, Stockings, Shoes." Beside each item that an individual child might have there was room for a description of the type of fabric or anything significant; the rest could be either left blank or crossed out. The final category at the bottom of the form, "Marks on the Body," left space for any non-clothing-related identifiers to be noted: a ribbon attached to the child's wrist, waist, or leg; a note pinned to the child; or even a coin or other token left with the child. Despite the standardization, the form was dependent on the inclinations of the particular agent filling it out; some left the clothing blank if there was a token, while others left detailed descriptions of every item included with a child. Some documented conversations with the person leaving the child while others carefully copied out the contents of a note rather than simply acknowledging its existence (see Figure 5).

While the institution only occasionally noted distinguishing marks on the infants' bodies as opposed to their clothing, for the most part, it was the parent or guardian who documented such marks in the letters they left with their children along with other information. For example, parents left writing describing various elements of their children's bodies: Child 323, a one-week-old girl, has a note that concludes, "The Child has a Currant Mark upon the left Eye" (Billet 323, Billet Book 4), while child 534, a seven-week-old boy, has a note that ends with "his Name is John Bayley he has a Mole under – his Right Eare In takeing of this poor Child the Aflicted Mother wil be Ever in Dutty bound to pray for you" (Billet 534, Billet Book 7). Other children have notes documenting a "Read Correll on the Left Side of his Nose" (Billet 652, Billet Book 8), or "a red mark upon the left Eye lash" (Billet 636, Billet Book 8).

The occasional exception to this general indifference in the billets to actual infant bodies was in the case of race, although that is complicated in several ways. Among the children whose race was noted in any way in the first fifteen years of the Foundling Hospital, it is the billet, not the parents' notes, that marks it. We do know that five children were identified on their billets as dark-skinned or somehow racialized from 1741 to 1751. All but the first child, whose entry was before standardized billets, were identified under "Marks on the Body" or "Marks and Cloathing of the Child" by the agent of the Hospital.

The first child to be identified by skin color is in 1741, in a phrase after an extended description of his clothes, where this "Male child about a week old" is described as "of a very tawny complexion." Like roughly half of the children, he was left with a note, described here as "a paper on the breast."[25] In 1743 and 1748, respectively, two children were identified as a "Moor": The first, a two-month-old named Miles Cook by the Hospital, was described as "Meanly dressd" (Billet 165, Billet Book 3), with the additional comment that "this Child was of a Dark olive complexion like a Moor has long black hair" (General Register, Volume 1, Child

---

[25] The note is pinned, folded, and sealed, and therefore illegible (Billet 75, Billet Book 1).

165). The second, another two-month-old boy, was described simply under "Marks on the Body" as "a Tawny moor very meanly Dressed" (Billet 448, Billet Book 6).[26] Two children, both of whom entered the Hospital in 1750, are given names that reflect their racialized identity. The two-month-old girl whose billet has no clothing description but simply the words "a Mulatto" under "Marks on the Body" (Billet 631, Billet Book 8) is given the name Jane Black (General Register, Volume 1, Child 631), while the six-week-old boy whose clothing is described is identified under "Marks and Cloathing of the Child" as "a Mulatto Male Child" (Billet 660, Billet Book 8) and is given the name Christian Moor (General Register, Volume 1, Child 660). With such a small set of examples from the first decade or so of the Hospital, it is hard to draw any conclusions. Were there other non-white children whose race was not marked on their billets? Were certain agents concerned about race while others were not? Were these children treated differently in their time at the institution? Perhaps the early years of the Foundling Hospital were racially mixed to such a degree that some agents did not see any reason to differentiate children of various races, or perhaps the Foundling Hospital was so racially homogenous that the five children with dark skin that passed through its doors in the first decade were carefully noted. Ultimately, the billets are an imperfect signal of the lives of the infants they tally, and the institution's relationship to those infant bodies is tantalizingly out of reach.

Tokens

While the billet is the institution's attempt to contain the earlier life of the child, it is the token kept with that billet that most fully evokes the relationship between birth parent and child. In the advertisements printed in newspapers on the eve of reception days, parents were instructed to leave an identifying object with their child: "All persons who bring children are requested to affix on each child some particular writing, or other distinguishing mark or token, so that the children may be known hereafter if necessary" (quoted in Brownlow 38). This is the "Paper, or Remarkable thing" that *An Account* has the Governors seal into the billet (*An Account* 61; Levene 55), which was to be an additional safeguard to identifying the (renamed and reclothed) child should she/he ever be retrieved by a parent. In fact, fewer than half the records included any kind of token; those that did are overwhelmingly written notes. And even though the Hospital instructs parents to bring such a thing, there is very little information for parents about what such an item might be, and so there is a significant range in the archive of "distinguishing mark[s] or token[s]."

---

[26] This child appeared in the General Register as "George Luba," dying May 14, 1749 (General Register, Volume 1, Child 448).

These tangible markers of loss and separation occupy a strange rhetorical space. Affixed to a child's body, they are the mother's final message not to her infant, but to the person she/he will become by way of the agents of an institution that requires their separation. However, these tokens, often lovingly prepared by the mothers, are stripped almost immediately from the child and sealed into a packet by order of the institution, never to be seen by the child. Interestingly, those sealed packets (billets with tokens attached to them) were opened at some point in the nineteenth century, long after the foundling in question would have died or moved on, and bound into books, which is the form they take in the archive – 202 leather-bound volumes of individual separation and loss. Together, the tokens and billets thus embody the tension between the anonymity offered to the parents by the institution and the desire of many of those parents to be known by the child. In particular, inscribed tokens, from barely legible scrawled notes to poems and other ornately scripted short letters, are an uneasy link between the child's past and the institution. They represent the parents' past connection and hoped-for future with their children, even if that possibility is vanishingly small for some.

Those tokens (notes, buttons, cloth, etc.) that remain serve as raw and often jarring attempts at connection produced, selected, and/or created by the parent, made all the more searing through the knowledge that they were instantly separated from the child and accounted for in files and records, never to be seen again by the child. The message contained in the token is often obscure; sometimes the letters/words are not clear, but more often the token is not visible as such. Perhaps it is a cherished ribbon, which out of the hands of the mother is simply a worn item of clothing. Embroidery on an item of clothing could have been handed down from a master or mistress, or it could have been lovingly inscribed for this specific infant. Separated from the parent and the name whose initials are inscribed, a token risks being passed over, lost, or misrecognized. Its meaning is contingent on a loving and familiar relationship.

Tokens are an evocative attempt to situate the child in its earlier life – albeit often in inscrutable ways. John Styles, who has written extensively on textile tokens, points out that children's clothes in this period were often made out of repurposed adult garments, usually the mother's. Fabric tokens are thus related to mothers and carry a particular intimacy (Styles *Threads of Feeling* 29). At the same time, ribbon (top knot and cockade), baby clothes (caps and sleeves), and embroidery all served as different kinds of remembrances that are not particularly legible to modern viewers.[27] Finally, written words (letters, other documents) and fabric/objects sometimes merge since ribbons had words

---

[27] See Styles, "Objects of Emotion," 167–68 on the "contextual and impermanent" emotional charge of tokens.

embroidered onto them and notes were constructed out of pasteboard and cut into shapes and symbols. Great care was sometimes taken in producing tokens, from the extensive sewing of pouches and other items, the occasionally refined language of notes, and even rubbing and engraving of metal coins and tags.

For modern readers, the paper tokens (as opposed to the objects) have a number of advantages. The most practical is that they were not separated from the billets, and so they can be connected to individual children as they maintain their presence in the billet books. Their words also give voice to the thoughts and desires of individual parents, and in that way produce limited agency for the parent(s). Even so, written notes have their own limitations. For those whose literacy skills were weak, for example, finding someone else to write a note could be a complicated business, and so even tokens that were not visibly marked by extensive effort might, in fact, have involved a great deal of hardship for parents. Because of the vagaries of the lottery system, the token left with the child had to be created even knowing the separation might not happen; it is therefore imaginable that many parents arrived not fully prepared for the final separation. This becomes especially visible on one particular date, November 12, 1742, when the Foundling Hospital unusually provided the opportunity for those leaving a child to write a note on-site if they had not brought one with them: of the twenty-four children admitted that evening, nineteen had a note, only six of which had been written before. In fact, only five of the children left on that day did not have a written note of some sort, although it is very possible that the children's clothing contained some kind of "distinguishing mark" that was not recognized as a token. This suggests that far more parents than those who came prepared with a note might have wanted to leave a message with or for their child.

Either because of limited access to writing utensils or simply a lack of facility, those whose literacy was constrained could find themselves silenced at the moment of separation. Of the notes identified as "paper wrote here" on that November evening, several had marks rather than words, suggesting that even parents with uncertain writing ability still chose to communicate something – anything – in this moment. Thus the parent of child 139, a two-month-old girl "Neatly Drest," left a paper with a large, shaky cross but no words – no blots, but quivering lines and two passes at the vertical line of the cross. Someone else recorded the time of entry: "3 qu past five a Clock" (Billet 139, Billet Book 2). Child 141, a two-month-old boy, was left with a folded note that says in one hand "St James parish" with a star/flower shape (four crossed lines) and a squiggle below; this strongly suggests that one wielder of the pen was not fully literate, but was leaving a mark for her child – blotted, uneven lines, uncertain marks – but certainly distinctive enough to retrieve a child if possible

(Billet 141, Billet Book 2). Another child, a five-week-old boy described as "Almost starvd – very meanly dressd" had a note marked with a blot and a squiggle (possibly an M) with words that are largely illegible (Billet 150, Billet Book 2). Several other children had such notes: one with a shape like a star (Billet 152, Billet Book 2); another with an attempted name beginning with a "p" whose letters are so poorly shaped that it is largely illegible (Billet 158, Billet Book 2); another with a shape that resembles a backward and sideways 4 whose lines are retraced and smudged (Billet 160, Billet Book 2). All have the notation "with a paper wrote here" and several of those papers have additional words on them, suggesting that agents of the Hospital helped fill out information for the parent(s) on this particular reception day.

Other days have the occasional inexpertly written mark, although not as many as on that exceptional November 1742 date. There were also other kinds of coded or imperfectly legible information; child 686, for example, had "Round the neck a black ribbon with a Thin piece of Pastboard tied to it" with the words "My name is Lenard, I was born Jan.^{ry} 8th 1750/1. at 7 of the Clock in the evening S.Q.M.G.S. – H.S.L.R. – L.B.S.H.R" (Billet 686, Billet Book 9). Perhaps initials, perhaps abbreviated words, the string of letters was a message understood only by the parent who might hope to retrieve the child someday. Although quite different from the shapes and squiggles of what were presumably nonliterate mothers, even carefully constructed notes remind us of the ways billets and tokens could remain illegible, maintaining the intimacy of a parent–child relationship even in this most publicly scarring moment.

Notes and other tokens all suggest a strong commitment on the part of the mothers to the possibility of reunion. As the advertisements placed in local papers made explicit, their function was to maintain the possibility of the return of the child to her/his birth parent. Any parent who left a token, then, believed in the possibility of reuniting with their child. If the notes that were present clearly indicated such a wish, the opposite is not always the case; children without tokens cannot necessarily be interpreted as unmarked or simply abandoned. For example, the notation on the billet for child 758 is revealing: "The Woman that brought this Child declar'd that ye Name of this Child was Samuel Green but she had left ye paper at home" (Billet 758, Billet Book 10). We can assume that for every instance this was noted there were a number where the circumstances did not offer the mother the opportunity to explain the absence of a token.

Of the notes left with children, the single most common was simply a name – presumably the child's name. Such notes were often the only record of the original name parents intended for their children. Once the note was sealed into the billet, the name (with its associated relations and family connections) was never uttered again. Instead, benefactors of the Foundling Hospital, as we have seen, had free reign to assign both a first and last name to each child, and they often did so with great relish. Surely Elizabeth Foundling (General Register, Volume 1, Child 209), Mary Mild (General Register, Volume 1, Child 293), and Hopegood Helpless (General Register, Volume 1, Child 306) struggled with names so dour. Most likely children with other kinds of extravagant names, whose significance was for benefactors, not children, struggled differently: Andrew Marvel (General Register, Volume 1, Child 90), Augustus Casar [sic] (General Register, Volume 1, Child 205), Robin Hood (General Register, Volume 1, Child 249), and Desdemona Courtly (General Register, Volume 1, Child 372) are scattered throughout the records; Peter Paul Reuben (General Register, Volume 1, Child 613) and Michael Angelo (General Register, Volume 1, Child 614) are beside each other in the General Register. Why benefactors assigned such grandiose names to children intended for servitude is not clear; they certainly didn't assign such names to their own children. When juxtaposed to the simpler names birth parents assigned their infants in their notes, the ways in which names signal attachment become hollowed out for foundlings.

Even lengthier notes often included repeated pleas to keep a child's name. For example, a ten-day-old child was accompanied by the following note: "this infant Has been baptized by a [illeg–covered] urch of England and Named George – [illeg–covered] over, Beg [illeg] ask'd for By that Name ... Agreable To the Rules of ye Hospitall" (Billet 53, Billet Book 1). Another child, about a month old, "Mary Abery is Chrisn – Buckelbery Parish in the County of Boasks if you Please to take Notice shall be Obligd" (Billet 277, Billet Book 4). In each case, the baptism gives additional weight to the desire to keep the name, and while the request is couched in polite language ("shall be obligd," "if you please," "I Beg"), the parent insists (fruitlessly) on the fixity of the identity. In cases where the infant has not been baptized, the desire for permanence in naming seems just as strong: "this Child is not baptized please to name it Mary Collins" (Billet 4, Billet Book 1), or "this child is not baptized & I desire he may be baptized & called Roger Brown" (Billet 1, Billet Book 1). Then there is the more deferential "I beg the child may be chris[tened] be the name of Ann Ford" (Billet 23, Billet Book 1), or "It is Humbly Begg'd That This Child be Christne'd Charly s^r name Lewis it was born the 22nd Decemb^r 1746" (Billet 286, Billet Book 4). In these cases, the child received a completely different name in the General Register, with neither the first nor last name requested by the parent reflected in the new name.

Children never saw the information left by their parents, even their own date of birth – sometimes even the hour of birth – specified in these notes. Children were thus stripped not only of the relationality that came with their birth names, but also any information that marked them as anything other than a foundling with a shared baptismal record of the institution, identical clothing with other foundlings, and an identifying number inscribed on a tag. The Foundling Hospital's policies thus often worked at odds with the stated desire of the parents, which was to fix their child's identity in connection to their origins either through the record of the moment of their birth or through a specific name, and often both. These markers made visible the particularity of each child in ways that parents knew but that the Hospital erased.

In fact, mothers often left clear instructions about how to individualize their child – certainly through a name, as we have seen, but also in other ways. Child 754, for example, had a note explaining that "The silver Groat put about this Child's Neck is as a Token that it may be known if enquired . . . it is desired that it may be kept always a[bout its] neck – the piece is Dated 1686 –marked with the Letters J.G. – "(Billet 754, Billet Book 10). Child 788 had a note specifying "It is humbly Desired that this Child Born June the 11th 1751 may be baptized by the name of Barnabas its sirname is [illegible] it is also beg'd that the Ear Ring may be kept in his Ear." The billet mentioned an "Earing on ye right Ear" (Billet 788, Billet Book 10). Both boys were left with sentimental tokens and specific instructions of their mothers that their unusual gestures would be made visible to their sons throughout their lives. In neither case did this in fact happen, as both children were separated from their tokens, and the child called by his mother Barnabas (Joseph Beebee in the General Register [General Register Volume 1, Child 788]) died within a year.

Even as mothers (fruitlessly) pleaded for their children to retain marks of their earlier identity such as names or specific items, agents of the Hospital were the only ones to see these parental tokens, and this bureaucratic audience was the main one that mothers increasingly communicated with through their tokens. Some of those requests were very general; they were simply the acknowledgment of a parent's desire to have the child be remarked. One child had a note saying, "This Child's name is Jane Ginaiver her parents being att this time unable to keep her desires ye favour of this house" (Billet 269, Billet Book 4). Another child had a note saying, "Mary Davenport Born May 20th 1750 Pray take a particular Care of her" (Billet 617, Billet Book 8). Slightly more unusual, child 427, a five-day-old boy, was left with the following note: "This Child was Born July the 3d: 1748 about two o'Clock in the Afternoon with this Caul o're his face which I desire may be preserved with the Writing. He is not yet Baptized and if it not contrary to the Rule of the House Should be Glad to have him called Wm Rabless or that name added to any other he may be called by. I am yours & J.R July ye 8th 1748." Under "Marks on the body," the following information was included: "a Letter pinned in a Clout upon the Breast with a piece of caul in the inside of the letter" (Billet 427, Billet Book

5). This fleshly reminder of the connection of mother and child was entered into the record, vividly disrupting the abstraction of this separation. More typically, a three-week-old boy simply had a blotted note written in awkwardly formed letters poignantly stating, "This Chald I desir you wold taat Car of" (Billet 846, Billet Book 11). Contained in these simple notes was the parents' conviction that their children's personhood was significant, although they were at a loss to verbalize why their particular child was special in ways that might matter to the Foundling Hospital. And that was the difficulty these parents faced; for the institution, their child was not special, or exceptional, or different. The separation marked a moment in which parents could only plead for some recognition of their child, some possibility that the child would understand her/himself as loved and worthy of care. We know that once the billet was sealed, those wishes were never conveyed to those children.

Many of the notes express concern about how parents will know their children should they be in a position to collect them at some later point. Once again, it is often the name that is the parent's choice for an identifier, although that choice is routinely ignored by the Foundling Hospital. Parents (rightly) were concerned that once the child's name was altered, the systems for recovering the child were unstable. They pleaded for memory, and the name became the child's token. One example left with child 278, evidently written by an inexperienced wielder of the pen, says:

> most [blot covers word] Gentalmen
> I [blot the?] hunhipe [unhappy] Mother of this child Am at this time ve[ry] poor but have A prospect of being beatter so shall be bound to pray for you if you will remark this Chilld In case i hope to call for it y[blot] not christened but i woled be glad to have it caalld william [blot]Giddy i beag your pardon [blot] A hope a mothers caring will pleed my exquse
> This child is a weak old to day being born the 26 of [cross out blot] September (Billet 278, Billet Book 4)

The mother here negotiates a curious sort of bargain; she will pray for the "Gentalmen" if they "remark this Chilld" as she hopes her circumstances will shift enough in the future to allow her to retrieve her child. She thus marks the separation as she prepares the way for a reunion, a common theme in a number of notes. Child 333 is left with a similar note: "Worthy gentleman I beg that you d take care of this Child for I am not In a compasity to mintan it but I hope it will soon be in my power to have It a gaine with pain the expence I hope you not refuss Its not yet named be plesed to let the name be William Parisatis July 18 1747" (Billet 333, Billet Book 4). Again, the note is addressed to the "gentleman" and the mother signals her ongoing commitment to her child through the stated hope that she will be in a position to take her child back. The hope that each child will maintain the name they were given becomes the focus of the retrieval: If they keep the name, they will be recoverable. Sadly in both cases, they neither kept their birth names nor were ever returned to their parents.

The expense that the mother in the second note mentions recurs in several other notes as well. Child 399, a three-week-old boy, has this note: "Wm Cross, the mother of the Child hath some Dependance hereafter this and w[ill] be glad to pay the expense of the house if Customary, and take the Child out again" (Billet 399, Billet Book 5), while child 564, another three-week-old boy, has this note: "I beag for God Sake that you will Take of this boy Till ye is 6 years of age & than ye money will be paid for him is name is John writ of higgale and on will call and see it often" (Billet 564, Billet Book 7). Sadly John (renamed Peter in the General Register) died eleven days after he was admitted (General Register, Volume 1, Child 564) while William (renamed Henry in the General Register) was never collected by his parents (General Register, Volume 1, Child 599).

Other notes offer a more generalized hope that the future will be better, and that however dire the circumstances are now, something will change. Child 681, a five-week-old baby girl (Billet 681, Billet Book 9), has the following note: "pleas to take care of this child by ye Name of Elizabeth Dobson fore I believe she may be called for." Another baby girl, child 424, has this note: "Gentelem your Patitinor Humbley begse Leafe the Childse name be as it is Crished [Christened] An[n] Lawrence it may be of Servise to the Child Hereafter" (Billet 424, Billet Book 5). The name in all these cases is an act of memory, both in the sense that the parent begs to have some small part in the child's identity in the future and in a vague sense that it "may be of service" to the child, if not in the direct retrieval by the parent, then at least in the possibility that someone else will step forward – but only if the child is recognizable.

In some of the notes, the request for care shifts from the child to the paper – as if, somehow, these are interchangeable. In this compact, care for the note ensures the return of the child to the parent. We see, for example, a three-week-old boy, "Neatly Drest," with a note saying, "This Childs name is Richard Baker and the Mother begs this paper may be kept that she may know her dear Child" (Billet 299, Billet Book 4). The child Elizabeth Townsin has a note that similarly asks for care for the note: "to the greandons of the foundling Hospital Gente^m The child baptized and her name Eliabeth Townsin be pleased that this paper may preserved so as to be produced with the child if Desires November the 10 1749" (Billet 559, Billet Book 7). Such phrasing is common; notes instruct "Its humbly requested this Paper Should be taken care of [the child] will be Inquired after in some time" (Billet 570, Billet Book 7), or "please to Lay this paper by that it may be produced with the child when called for" (Billet 605, Billet Book 8). These notes acknowledge that while the child will grow and change, the note remains stable, and as time passes, it is the crucial conduit to the reconnection of the parent and child.

There is even the occasional attempt to use poetry to contain the excess of emotion in these tokens. Scholar Laura Schattschneider writes of the intersection of literature and the practices of the Foundling Hospital, and her article points to the ways tokens both participated in and produced a particular rhetoric of child abandonment in eighteenth-century Britain. Multiple novels featuring foundlings were popular in this period, and the rhetorical flourishes of poetry, or even of Latin inscription reflecting the general fascination with lost and abandoned children, made their way into the tokens left with infants. Such tokens as well as the complex embroidery and other creative elements of material objects produce a vocabulary of loss for the women leaving their children, one that Schattschneider points out both obscures and engages with the trope of the fallen woman. A note written in elegant handwriting and connected to an infant boy brought to the Hatton Garden location of the Hospital was written in verse (after an opening introduction), and makes this visible. One of a handful of poems among the notes of the first decade of the Hospital, it reads as follows:

> St Andrews Holborn 17th April, 1741
> I was Born in this Parish on Tuesday 24th February last & have been Christened in the said Church by the name of Thomas, Soe my name is Tho.s Lay"
>
> Pray use me well & you shall find
> My Father will not prove unkind
> Unto that Nurse who,s my protector
> Because he is a Benefactor
>
> Wether ye Child live or die
> be please to send an aco.t thereof
> to ye Jamaica Coffee house
> in St Michaels alley, in one
> months Time Directed to M:J
> it will be acknowledge[d a] great Favour
>
> (Billet 38, Billet Book 1)

The first two sections of the note are written in the first person in the voice of the infant boy, with the specificity of the date of birth, insistence on a name, and insistence on the particularity of the child that we have seen in so many other notes. In an interesting gambit, the writer here juxtaposes the nurse as his protector with his father as a benefactor. The phrasing is curious: Is the poem suggesting the birth father is one of the wealthy benefactors of the hospital? Is he likely to give money to the institution? Is this a mother's attempt to plead for kindness to her child by hinting at his powerful father? The poem suggests a direct transactional consequence for the specific nurse in relation to the baby boy identified by his mother as Thomas Lay, even though the processes of the Hospital will alter that name and mask that identity.

The shift in the last "stanza" ruptures the fiction of the child speaking and instead becomes the plea of the mother; in that shift, the posturing of power and connections is broken. As with so many of the parents cited throughout, "M:J" here simply wants to know: Does her child have a better life in the Hospital? Has her baby boy survived, and does this mother have the right any more to ask for information about her child? Like so many of the other mothers to follow, she asks knowing that whatever her intentions to visit or inquire or reimburse the institution, this moment of rupture is almost certainly permanent, and in an age of high infant mortality exacerbated by the difficult circumstances that have led to this separation, the likelihood of ever reuniting with her child, whatever assurances are made in the note, are vanishingly small.

Grief is contained here within the ritual, formal language of poetry, while the imperfect rhyme of "protector" and "benefactor" as well as the shift in and out of the poetic meter suggests some of the imbalance and inadequacy of the form. The note reveals a creative impulse – a way to contain the well of pleading, obsequious despair even as it marks out identity, connection, and closeness between the birth parents and the child. The final formal language of "it will be acknowledged a great favor" technically refers to the information to be left at the coffeehouse, but it also gestures toward the larger transaction and the supplicant position of the mother for the child that is no longer hers.

As modern onlookers, we are shut out from some of the most important elements of this agonizing moment of separation; we don't know the mindset of the parents and the reasons for the separation. We don't know in most cases what specific economic or personal circumstances led to this moment, and we often don't even know who left the child. The mother? A city or state official? Father or other family member? Friend or neighbor? However, there is an undeniable fascination with the tangible reminders of this moment, the tokens left by desperate parents. Certainly, the audiences passing through the Foundling Hospital Museum today feel it, and these tokens have been on display in one form or another since the nineteenth century, suggesting that the fascination is not new. On any given day, museum goers linger by the array of tokens, drawn by the heartbreak as well as the possibility that each token embodies the commitment to reunification between parent and child. These tokens reveal the tension within the records between the affection and individuality recognized by the mother, and the systems, rules, and consistency required by the institution. The mother marks the individuality of her child and/ or her relationship with that child through the token while the institution encloses it, files it, and then transforms that infant body into something different: a commodity. In the moment of separation, infants are transformed from individuated persons to "object(s) of charity" while the objects left with them are sealed away. As the child matures into the laborer that the institution is designed to produce, those marks of individuality and difference are traded for a pleasing sameness and regimentation in the uniformed bodies living and working in rows.[28]

2 Foundlings

Nursing the Foundling

If the tokens left by parents plead for memory and a sense of the individuality of each child, the goals of the Foundling Hospital were more about systems, structures, and regimentation. Ideally, within a week of being admitted, children were sent out to the country with a wet nurse; they were carried away by their nurses, along with a regulation-issue bundle of clothes, a receipt, and a pewter tag attached around their necks (not to be removed). They returned to the Foundling Hospital years later at the instruction of the General Committee. The Foundling Hospital is clear about the relationship between the nurse and her charge; there is payment for services rendered, with a bonus for keeping a child alive longer than a year (Berry, 57).

The parental relationship, at times characterized by the token and ruptured on the reception day, is replaced by a transactional one with the child's assigned wet nurse, who is controlled and managed through the centralized Foundling Hospital.[29] Today, we might identify the relationship between the wet nurse and the child as a loosely defined foster situation, but that is not entirely accurate. It was more properly a paid position through which the policies of the Hospital

---

[28] The materials published by the Foundling Museum focus on the tokens and their history: Bright and Clark, *Introduction to the Tokens* discusses metal and other types of tokens connected to individual children; John Styles's *Threads of Feeling* focuses on textile tokens, as does his short essay, "Objects of Emotion." *The Foundling Hospital: An Introduction* reproduces several of the tokens among its images, and the website for the Foundling Hospital Museum has an extensive selection of tokens and their individual histories for viewing. Robert Pinsky's poetic tribute to the foundling tokens appears in *The American Scholar*.

[29] Some of the children admitted to the Foundling Hospital were there precisely because there *was* no maternal relationship; notes written by friends, neighbors or parish officials mention the death of the mother or the abandonment of the child by both parents (Billet 676, Billet Book 8) (see footnote 22). It is generally the case, however, that the reception day was overwhelmingly about the separation of the child from her/his birth mother.

were enacted. Certainly, some were loving relationships that were mutually rewarding. We know that for all the attempts to render the nurse–child relationship purely transactional, there were recurring mentions of affection between foster families and the infants they had raised. And as others have pointed out, foster families made several attempts to formalize an ongoing relationship with their charges through indenture and other means.[30] However, by and large the transaction was supervised by agents of the Hospital – in this case, inspectors – and was seen less as an alternative family than as a strategy for extending the lives of children who were otherwise almost certain to die.

Throughout their childhood, the influence of the institution was ever present, what Miley and Read characterize as "accounting"; unlike other small children, they lived in families as part of a financial arrangement, were dressed in clothes provided for them by the Foundling Hospital, and had a number fastened to them at all times (173). Perhaps lovingly integrated into a family unit or kept at arm's length by caretakers fully aware of how transitory the relationship would be, this arrangement stands for the first few years of their lives, at which point children "are to be returned by the Inspectors of the Hospital, together with all the Cloathing belonging to them. And the Steward is to give the Inspectors Receipts for the same" (*An Account* 67; Levene 58). Their existence as "objects of charity" is clear in the exchange of receipts and tags and clothing; their bodies are one item among many that are part of the larger transactional processes of charity that the General Committee oversaw.

The inspectors (a surprising number of whom were women), served as a conduit between the institution and the child, managing the exchange of goods and information with the nurses, who raised their assigned child through the early years in their own families for a fee.[31] The accounting here is done through the numbers affixed to the children: "Above all Things, the Inspectors are to observe, that the Numbers fastened to the Children be not taken off, and if, by any Accident, they should be broke off, they are to seal them on with their own Seals, that this may be an Evidence, that the Children are not changed" (*An Account* 67; Levene 58). Inspectors were to be as mindful of the clothing as of the babies; they "are to be particularly cautious ... not to suffer any Alteration of the Fashion of the Cloathing allowed by the Hospital and to take Care, that

---

[30] For more on this relationship, see Kate Gibson "Fostering the Foundlings"; Claire Phillips "Child Abandonment in England, 1741–1834," 2 and 6; McClure 129–32; and Berry 114–16. See also Lydia Clay-White's informative article "Nurses and Inspectors at the Foundling Hospital" on the Coram website: https://coramstory.org.uk/explore/content/blog/nurses-and-inspectors-at-the-foundling-hospital.

[31] According to Lydia Clay-White, approximately 40 percent of inspectors in the mid eighteenth century were women: https://coramstory.org.uk/explore/content/blog/nurses-and-inspectors-at-the-foundling-hospital.

the old Cloathing be returned to the Hospital, as soon as new Cloathing is sent them, which ought to be annually only" (*An Account* 66; Levene 58).

The records in the digital archive related to this moment in the process can be difficult to access; the listing of Nursery books doesn't start until June 1756, which marks the beginning of the General Reception period, while the Inspection books, which start in 1749, are organized by region, and are often sparsely filled in. The text that most fully discusses this period in the infant's life is actually quite distant from it. *An Essay upon Nursing* by William Cadogan, originally published in 1748 and reissued throughout the eighteenth century, was conceived and published for the benefit of the Foundling Hospital. Just as *An Account* framed the original separation of the child from her/his birth family, this text reframed and reorganized this intensively maternal moment (albeit a financially negotiated foster situation rather than a biological connection) in terms of patriarchy. However imperfectly this document captured the details of the early years in the country, at least from the Hospital's perspective, it was the guidebook to child-rearing; the subcommittee minutes of April 12, 1749, indicate that "all the Children be sent into the Country to wet Nurses under the inspection of some Person of Character and Fortune in the Neighbourhood, and that they remain there until they are three years old, and that during that Time, their Diet, Clothing, &c. be conformable to the directions given in a Treatise entitled an Essay upon Nursing and the Management of Children for their Birth to three years old" (Sub-Committee Minutes, Volume 1, page 27). Cadogan, then, defined the philosophical underpinnings of this period of childcare.

Cadogan's *An Essay upon Nursing* was originally published anonymously in London "by a physician ... by Order of the General Committee for transacting the Affairs of the [Foundling] Hospital" (this is the edition reprinted in Levene 95). Modern scholars have been drawn to what most consider the more humane practices that he advocates: looser clothing for infants, maternal breastfeeding for the first year, and more freedom for babies and toddlers to explore their worlds. Along the way they overlook the masculinist model at the heart of Cadogan's suggestions; his theories are predicated on a contempt for the misguided women who have up to then controlled child-rearing.[32] He is thus part of a larger trend in the eighteenth century of men replacing women's traditional knowledge in various spheres, most notably physicians replacing midwives in birthing spaces. And for all of his contempt, it is clear that there is tension between his ideal and the reality on the ground – we know, for example,

---

[32] See Shchuka, "Nursed under his own Eye" for a more sympathetic perspective on Cadogan's essay, and Johnston, "Big Mother" and Perry, "Colonizing the Breast" for a considerably less positive perspective.

that the clothes sent out with the children do not conform to Cadogan's recommendations, children stayed in the countryside considerably longer than three years, and it is highly unlikely that the wet nurses (most of whom lived very modest lives in rural England) would have read the essay or concerned themselves with its suggestions.

Cadogan characterizes his essay as a "few loose Thoughts on the Subject of Nursing Children" (*An Essay* 34; Levene 112) directed as a letter to "one of the Governors of the Foundling Hospital" (*An Essay* title page; Levene 95); he modestly concludes the essay with "If you think it may be of any Use to publish this Letter, I am not unwilling it should appear; if not, do with it what you please. I deliver it up as a Foundling to be disposed of as you think proper" (*An Essay* 34; Levene 112). The text, then holds an interesting position; as a "foundling" it exists in relationship to the Hospital "to do with it what you please"; it has no authority or status outside the control of the General Committee. However, as the product of "a Physican" (even an anonymous one), it does in fact carry a great deal of authority, and so one voice of authority (the Foundling Hospital) reinforces that of another (a physician). Most significantly, the text/foundling replaces the infant/foundling as the true product of the Hospital, and its words offer to reshape child-rearing not only within the Hospital, but for all children across the British empire. By equating the publication of his book with a mother's difficult choice to give up her child, Cadogan reveals to us how abstracted his thoughts are on the issues at the institution's center.

An Essay opens with a clear focus on the masculinist rhetoric that runs through the entire pamphlet: "It is with great Pleasure I see at last the Preservation of Children become the Care of Men of Sense: It is certainly a Matter that well deserves their Attention, and, I doubt not, the Publick will soon find the good and great Effects of it" (*An Essay* 3; Levene 97). It certainly seems that gender norms are a pressing problem here. Women have been left to their own devices in raising babies, Cadogan suggests, and it's high time men intervened more forcefully. He writes, "In my Opinion, this Business has been too long fatally left to the Management of Women, who cannot be supposed to have proper Knowledge to fit them for such a Task, notwithstanding they look upon it to be their own Province." The Foundling Hospital will save far more children by "introducing a more reasonable and more natural Method of Nursing," Cadogan assures his readers (*An Essay* 3; Levene 97), than it will by accepting infants into the care of the institution. Reason, in relation to nursing, is the province of "men of sense" – never women. With various juxtapositions Cadogan makes his point clear; masculine words like "Business" and "Management" as well as "Knowledge" and "reason" have been distressingly attached to women, with "fatal" consequences. Rather than givers of life, in Cadogan's version, women cause the death and suffering of infants through their poor management and mistaken ideas. In fact, he continues, "the Treatment of Children in general is wrong, unreasonable and unnatural," and when adults are in poor physical condition, it is "chiefly owing to bad Nursing, and bad Habits contracted early" (*An Essay* 5–6; Levene 98). Women, in this iteration, are not only responsible for the fatal mismanagement of child-rearing, but this mismanagement is the cause of poor health at every stage of life. He concludes this argument with the following sweeping statement: "that the present Method of Nursing is wrong, one would think needed no other Proof than the frequent Miscarriages attending it, the Death of Many and ill Health of Those that survive" (*An Essay* 8; Levene 99).

Cadogan acknowledges that "When a Man takes upon him to contradict received Opinions and Prejudices sanctified by Time, it is expected he should bring valid Proof of what he advances" (*An Essay* 5; Levene 98). His proof will be the children of the Foundling Hospital, who will not only be saved from the terrible fate their circumstances brought them to, but will also serve as models to the world of his new system. Because the Foundling Hospital children will be brought up "in a plain and simple Manner," he writes with great assurance, "when these Advantages appear in Favour of Children so brought up, as I am confident in time they will, it may serve to convince most Nurses, Aunts, Grandmothers &c. how much they have hitherto been in the wrong" (*An Essay* 5; Levene 98). With the oversight of the Governors, the steward, and all the men who form the governing body of the institution, Cadogan suggests enthusiastically, the authority of women in child-rearing will be completely done in.

A central element of Cadogan's theory is that men must scrupulously oversee the nursing practices of women. In particular, Cadogan argues, "I would earnestly recommend it to every Father to have his Child nursed under his own Eye, to make use of his own Reason and Sense in superintending and directing the Management of it" (*An Essay* 24; Levene 107). Cadogan juxtaposes the "squalling Brat" unsupervised by its father with the properly nursed and supervised child who "would be always quiet, in good Humour, ever playing, laughing, or sleeping" (*An Essay* 24; Levene 107). Cadogan's masculine system would do away with the unpleasantness of child-rearing, which he attributes to women's false ideas. Most importantly, it would take away all decision-making from mothers and instead insist on the innate superiority of fathers to make decisions about the bodies of their wives and babies.

He adds querulously that women's engagement with babies continues to be misguided as they grow. He complains, "It would not be ... amiss to forward their speaking plain, by speaking plain distinct Words to them, instead of the

Namby Pamby Stile, and giving them back their own broken inarticulate Attempts; by which means, I believe, some Children scarecely speak intelligibly at seven Years of Age. I think they cannot be made reasonable Creatures too soon" (*An Essay* 33–34; Levene 111). When women speak in baby talk to their children rather than as reasonable adults, Cadogan suggests, they are stunting their children's development rather than engaging with them on an emotional level.

Cadogan concludes triumphantly, "If this Plan of Nursing were literally pursued, if the Children kept clean and sweet, tumbled and tos'd about a good deal, and carried out every Day in all Weathers; I am confident, that ... most Children would become healthy and strong, ... and very soon shift for themselves" (*An Essay* 21; Levene 105–06). Under his system there is no crying, no disease, no discomfort. His philosophy involves a stripping away of everything – clothing, feeding, maternal relations, history (misguided aunts, grandmothers, and nurses) – and replacing these with a "natural" model based on masculine reason and good sense that would lead to children's early self-sufficiency: precisely the logic of the Foundling Hospital.

However, if Cadogan's essay has as its goal the transformation of childcare, there is a clear tension between the ideal established in this text and the actual practice of the Foundling Hospital. Even in its broadest strokes, Cadogan's argument cannot align with the Hospital. Cadogan advocates for mothers to breastfeed their own babies, but of course the Foundling Hospital severs that relationship, sending infants instead to wet nurses in the countryside. He also advocates for a greater role for fathers in the earliest days of an infant's life, encouraging fathers to oversee breastfeeding. Again, the effect of the Foundling Hospital was to sever infants from their birth families, which means that Cadogan's theories of child-rearing cannot be enforced for the foundlings for whom he is ostensibly writing his manifesto. It becomes quite clear that the text was never really intended for the infants under its care but is instead intended for the benefactors of the Hospital; the foundlings are the cautionary tale that can make wealthy parents even more successful. They are the conduit to right living that someone like Cadogan can offer his clients.

Perhaps it is because the poverty often forcing the separation between parents and infants is so abstracted for Cadogan that he can make some of the claims he does in his treatise. He writes, for example, that poverty is an asset since there is less likelihood of overwhelming an infant with excess (*An Essay* 7; Levene 99). He complains that "Children in general are over-cloath'd and over-fed, and fed and cloath'd improperly. To these Causes I impute almost all their Diseases" (*An Essay* 9; Levene 100). This is a far cry from the infants brought in on reception days, most heartbreakingly child 33, characterized as "almost without clothes" (Billet 33, Billet Book 1). The Daily Committee minutes from the first reception day on March 26, 1740, mention that "many of [the children] appeared as if Stupifyed with some Opiate, and some of them almost Starved, One as in the Agonies of Death thr'o want of Food, too weak to suck, or to receive Nourishment" (Daily Committee Minutes and House Committee Minutes, page 7). Far from an asset, poverty is the cause of these separations, and surely no parent giving up a child would have seen the positive side of their situation.

As enlightened as some of Cadogan's practical ideas about nursing and clothing babies appear today, ultimately, his text is an exercise in dominance – masculine control over women and maternity. Cadogan's "foundling," as he calls his book, rhetorically replaces actual infants with a text, creating a slippage between the human and the principle, the body and the text. Cadogan is confident in his rightness, sweeping aside generations of lived experience and tradition with his certainty in his own ideas. As a father, he reasons, he has every authority to weigh in on a mother's experience. The text produces the moment farthest from the supervision of the male Governors of the Hospital as one best managed by men, thereby reaffirming the parenting model of the Foundling Hospital. The real work of maintaining children, says Cadogan, echoing *An Account*, is not in the actual regular work of feeding, clothing, and tending infants since these can all get managed for a fee – it is instead in documentation and supervision as well as in developing an abstract philosophical perspective, which, if done properly, will result in clean and happy children separated from the false ideas of women. When women give up their control over the early years of child-rearing and acknowledge the true authority of men in all such matters, Cadogan assures us, the world will be a better place.

While Cadogan's text, like *An Account*, was endorsed by the Hospital, the records embedded in the archive challenge the assurance of that model. Cadogan dismissed women's perspectives, although in practice Hospital structures were entirely dependent on women, from the matron and nurses employed by the institution to the wet nurses fostering in the countryside and the high numbers of women inspectors overseeing children's care. Even some of the men who might be inclined to embrace Cadogan's view demurred; one note in The London Archive (not digitized) rather comically skewers his observations. The anonymous author writes that upon reading Cadogan's book he queried the matron at the Foundling Hospital about this new method of feeding and dressing infants. He goes on to say:

> you may imagine I was a little surpris'd to find she seem'd puzzled at my question, & told me she knew of no alteration from their former method: that

their dress which I desired to see, was the same it had always been, that the young Children were all nurs'd in the country, & that the inspectors cou'd best give an acct if any alteration had been made in their feeding: but that in their dress or Cloathing none had been made, for that she gave out to the nurses the same things exactly as formerly.

He then skewers the gendered condescension of Cadogan's book:

I own I was greatly disappointed, expecting to have rally'd my wife out of half at least of her Childs cloathing: whilst she on the contrary turn'd the tables upon me, & cry'd out, ay, ay, my dear, Tis like the men, they are fond of novelty, Thought it a pritty thing, talk'd of it, recommended it, & then – thought no more of it. I fancy, Sir, a Committee of Women wou'd not be useless there & offer it to your & their consideration, for I verily believe Sr our great Grandmothers, & Grandmothers were very good Nurses & very good Housewives. (The London Archive, A/FH/A/06/001/002)

The letter upends Cadogan's wiltingly insulting assumptions about women's inability to reason, instead accusing men of chasing novelty and "pritty thing[s]." In this version, the writer is at the mercy of his wife, who immediately dismisses the contributions of men in this case, suggesting that a "Committee of Women" would do a far better job than these flighty men. The letter has a notation that it was read in the subcommittee on January 31, 1749. In the minutes for that day is a dry final comment – "The Subcommittee took into consideration the Dress of the Young Children and were of the Opinion that there is at Present no Occasion to make any Alteration therein" – suggesting that whatever the philosophical underpinnings of Cadogan's text, ultimately the gentlemen deferred to the nurses and matrons (and perhaps disgruntled wives) who recommended clothing for children (Subcommittee Minutes, Volume 1, page 55). However marginalized women were from the official pages of the institution, in practice, they were at its center.

Children's Lives in the Foundling Hospital

The most significant shift in the child's lived experience was the transition from rural life in a family to an institutional setting. The early years in the countryside, whether they were the idealized version that Cadogan offered ("always quiet, in good Humour, ever playing, laughing, or sleeping" from *An Essay* 24; Levene 107) or a more rough-and-tumble existence in largely impoverished rural communities, ended with the return to the Foundling Hospital in London. Since the first children were received into the Hospital in March 1741, at least some of them had returned to Hatton Garden before moving to the dormitories of the permanent buildings in Lamb's Conduit Field in late 1745.

In the early years, the children returned to London around the age of four or five until they were sent out to apprentice between the ages of nine and twelve, which generally translated for most children to at least five years in the institution.[33] This part of the child's life, the most extensive engagement for each child with the actual institution, is laid out in *An Account*, but also in very different ways in the apprentice materials as well as the hymns and other notes and administrative records that tell us more about the lives and expectations for the children in the institution. These years were largely defined by a fixed routine and constant reminders in various forms of the children's lowly status and limited options in the world. In every possible way, the Hospital emphasized that the children who survived infancy were to be menial laborers, and their labor made them useful citizens; every aspect of their life in the institution reinforced for them the conditions of that utility.

As we have seen, from the moment they were accepted as foundlings, the children's lives were clearly demarcated by their relationship with the institution. The shift in the nature of this relationship upon their return to London was marked both practically and symbolically through different clothing: "the returned Children are to be cloathed, in a Manner proper for Labour, and differing from that of the Children at Nurse; and their Number is to be fixed to their Cloaths, in some Manner, so as to be always visible, that every Child may be easily known thereby" (*An Account* 68; Levene 59). Furthermore, the children "are to be entered in a Book (divided into the different Wards of the Hospital) to be kept in the Ward into which they are ordered" (*An Account* 68; Levene 59). Just as the billet and General Register imagined children as records and numbers, upon their return to London they were once again turned into a notation in a book and a number through which to be tracked. Most importantly, they were to internalize an understanding of themselves as laborers with a profound obligation of gratitude toward their benefactors.

The Hospital maintained responsibility for children until they were discharged, and for children unable to work, the hospital managed their care until death. The physical labor of the children served two purposes: training for their futures and cutting the costs of operating the Hospital. The general expectation was that boys were "to be sent to Sea or Husbandry except so many as may be necessary to be employed in the Garden belonging to the Hospital, which is intended to be enlarged in such a manner as to supply the House and parts adjacent with vegetables, and to have in readiness Boys instructed in Gardening for such Persons as may incline to take them into their Service"

---

[33] By the mid 1750s, auxiliary hospitals were established to manage the influx of babies and also to provide space for older children. See "Branch Foundling Hospitals" by Chris Jones on the Coram website, at https://coramstory.org.uk/explore/content/article/branch-foundling-hospitals.

(Sub-Committee Minutes, Volume 1, page 28). Girls were to be "Instructed and Employed in all sorts of Household Work in Kitchen, Laundry and Chambers, to make them fit for Service; and at other times in Sewing Knitting and Spinning" in anticipation of their later work (Sub-Committee Minutes, Volume 1, page 20).

The children were expected to abide by a rigid schedule, with hours differentiated for summer and winter, although their daily tasks remained the same (Sub-Committee Minutes, Volume 1, page 129). The children rose at 5:00 in the summer (7:00 in the winter), and were expected to be out of the ward, fully dressed in their uniforms, in short order. The girls were then to assist the ward nurses in cleaning the rooms and making sure the beds were made "and every Thing in Order," while the boys were assigned work on the grounds, either in the garden or wherever they were needed for such tasks as "Digging, Houghing, Plowing with ploughs, manageable without Horses, Hedging, Cleaving Wood, Carrying Burthens, and such like Employments." At 8:00 (9:00 in the winter), they stopped for breakfast for an hour, after which they continued their work until noon. At that point they got two hours for "Dinner and Rest," after which they returned to work until 6:00 (or until dark in the winter). Reading instruction happened after this, until 8:00 at night, when the children had supper, after which (at 9:00) they went to bed.[34] All children at the Foundling Hospital were taught to read, although the allotment of time made the priority clear; the overwhelming amount of time was spent on labor, while only a small amount of time was spent on reading instruction (*An Account* 68–70; Levene 59–60).[35] Food was "plain and good of the sort," but no butter was allowed, "nor Strong Drink, Tea, Coffee, and Tobacco," ensuring that children did not partake of any indulgences at the Hospital. On Saturdays and public holidays, "they may be allowed to divert themselves with such Exercises, as will increase their Strength, Activity, and Hardiness," which meant that even their leisure was intended to condition them for lives of labor (*An Account* 70–71; Levene 60).

In addition to the daily schedule, children were taught in various ways how to understand their relation to the world, the institution, and their benefactors. One example is the daily prayers included in the Sub-Committee minutes for December 1753 for the use of the children. These morning and evening prayers so perfectly captured the expectations of the Hospital that 2,000 copies were distributed to inspectors in the country "to be taught the Children under their Inspection" and also "pasted on Boards in the several Wards of this Hospital, and be taught the Children by their Nurses" (Sub-Committee Minutes, Volume

---

[34] See also McClure 72–74.

[35] More attention was given to schooling after the first decade of the institution: Berry notes that a schoolmaster was hired in 1757, at which point the boys were instructed in writing (126). See also Pugh 63–67 and McClure 47–48.

1, page 207). These prayers reinforced for the children that they should understand themselves as constantly monitored (by God) in every thought and action, and that to live a good life they should be "strictly temperate & chaste," carefully govern their passions, and correct themselves "in every vicious Inclination." The prayer then reminds children to be "dutiful to my Governors & those who are put over me" and instructs them to "Bless my Governors, Friends, and Benefactors; and so provide for them and me here, that we may not be tempted to any Action contrary to our Duty" (Sub-Committee Minutes, Volume 1, page 207). In this way, from earliest childhood, the foundlings were trained to understand that their happiness was completely intertwined with that of the institution and the Governors and benefactors who shaped it. The labor of the children was not only physical, it was religious as well: a foundling life lived well included daily prayers for the salvation of Governors and benefactors as well as self-monitoring for right actions.

The staff (nurses, teachers, gardeners, stewards, etc.) who were their primary points of contact were also defined by their connection to the institution. For the duration of their employment at the Foundling Hospital, their entire lives were consumed by the overlapping needs of infants, young children, and those about to head out to their apprenticeship placement. Certainly, the Hospital was their workplace, but they were expected to live within its confines, as closely monitored as the children they oversaw. Various rules limited their days, with the steward and the matron as the central figures of authority over the daily activities of the Hospital. Together, the matron and the steward were responsible for managing the logistics of the entire lifespan of the children in relation to the Hospital, from their initial arrival as infants to their final departure, either through death or discharge. The steward "is to confine himself entirely to the Business of the Hospital, and never to be absent from it without Leave of the General Committee, President, Vice-President, or Treasurer, or Two of the Governors, who attended at the last Meeting" (*An Account* 48; Levene 47). In addition to overseeing the male servants, the steward was also responsible for managing the reception day, ensuring everything was in order, and he read the appointed prayers to the children and the household every morning and evening (*An Account* 49; Levene 48). The matron too was expected to live in the house and not have her own family; it was her responsibility to "inspect the Children, at the Time of their Reception; to have the immediate care of the Nurses, Children, and Female Servants; to see that proper Food be provided for the Children; and to have the Custody, and Care, of all Linnen, Wearing Apparel, Bedding, and Furniture, and of all Things necessary for the Female Servants" and of course the children (*An Account* 51; Levene 48–49). The steward and the matron were most directly responsible for ensuring that the mandates of the General Committee were properly enacted and for informing the General Committee of any issues affecting the children, from poor-quality clothing to unsatisfactory meals or disruptive behavior of children or lesser servants.

The focus of the institution through 1748 was primarily on training children to do the essential work of the Hospital itself, thereby limiting the number of servants needed to maintain the gardens, prepare the food and clothing for the children, and do the laundry and mending. Living quarters for the children thus merged their comfort and safety with their work training, and dormitories shared space with workrooms. Tasks were rotated so that the work was distributed most effectively for the efficiency of the Hospital itself and so that children developed various skills useful to their working lives. For example, the boys helped the girls with "mangling" the laundry less to develop their skills than to help with moving and lifting enormous loads of the "Linnen of the Hospital" while girls rotated through the kitchen and the laundry to develop a fuller range of skills (Sub-Committee Minutes, Volume 1, page 241). While the plan for the longer term was to apprentice the children out, at least initially the focus was on managing the Hospital's immediate needs – including discovering items that could be sold easily by the Hospital that showcased the skills of the children, whether that was netting for the boys or purses for the girls.

Once both wings were built children were separated by gender, as ordered in the Sub-Committee minutes for February 1752 in a sign of the increasing discomfort with the intermingling of boys and girls, which up to that time had been the norm (Sub-Committee Minutes, Volume 1, pages 127 through 130). Each wing had three floors and housed not just the children but also the staff of the Hospital, who were divided into the two wings by gender. The boys' wing was overseen by the steward and had just one room for the children on the main floor – a dining room – while much of it was given over to the grander rooms for visiting Governors and benefactors. The upper floor included the rooms for the chaplain, steward, clerk, and secretary, as well as a ward for the largest boys next to a workroom for the netmaker. The attic had an apothecary room, as well as a dormitory for the smaller boys and an infirmary, one storeroom for nets, thread, and twine, and another for seeds, dried herbs, and tools for the garden and malt for brewing (Sub-Committee Minutes, Volume 1, page 127).

The girls' wing, overseen by the matron, also had a dining room on the main floor, at the end of which was a schoolroom. On the other side of that space was the matron's parlor. The next floor was largely given over to dormitories: a large room for the smallest girls, which had twenty small beds for the girls and two large beds for the nurses, and a longer room for the bigger girls, also with twenty smaller beds for the girls and two larger beds for the school mistresses. The east room was the matron's, and the west room was a purse-maker's school for the girls and smallest boys. The attic had an infirmary, a storeroom, and a clothing room. The garrets had room for the country nurses passing through to pick up their infants, as well as space for cooks, housemaids, and laundry maids, while the courtyard on the women's side had a bakehouse, laundry, and washhouse while the one on the men's side had a brewhouse (Sub-Committee Minutes, Volume 1, pages 127 and 128). The dormitories and dining halls merged with storage spaces as the work the children were expected to take on, from gardening to rope making for the boys and cleaning, sewing, and laundry for the girls, was folded into their everyday lives.

The Sub-Committee Minutes from 1748 suggest some of the ongoing concerns about ensuring the best possible use of children's labor. This was the point at which the first sets of children (the first group had been admitted as infants in 1741) were coming to an age when they could be properly useful, and the anxiety around their early training was palpable (Sub-Committee Minutes, Volume 1, pages 1 through 21). The oldest of the children would have been around seven, and they were put to work at the hospital – the boys "winding silk" (this later shifted to hemp and then gardening) and the girls "making and mending Linnen" for all the children (including the babies in the country), which later expanded to household work as well as knitting, sewing, and spinning (*An Account*, xiii, xv, xvii–xviii, xx; Levene 13, 16). A year later, the Sub-Committee Minutes of April 12, 1749, listed the activities for boys and girls of specific ages; when the youngest children returned to the Hospital, they were to "be taught to read, to learn the Catechism &c and at proper intervals exercised in the open Air and Employed in such a manner as may contribute to their Health and induce a habit of activity, hardiness and Labour" (Sub-Committee Minutes, Volume 1, page 28). From age six to age twelve, the boys were to "be employed in making of Nets, spinning of Packthread twine and small Cordage; adapted to their several Ages and Strength, and that they mend their own Clothes Stockings &c." The minutes from January 1752 catalogued the ages of the boys and their various employments at the Hospital, from working in the garden to making netting, winding twine, filling needles, and making purses (Sub-Committee Minutes, Volume 1, page 77).

The girls were "employed in common Needle work, Knitting, and Spinning; and in the Kitchen, Laundry, and Household work, in order to make them useful servants to such proper persons as may apply for them; except so many as may be necessary to be employed in the Hospital; It being intended to have no other Female Servants in the Hospital, but Persons brought up therein, when they arrive to proper Ages" (Sub-Committee Minutes, Volume 1, page 28). In 1752, the ages of the girls and the work they were assigned to (kitchen, laundry, and "plain-work," or various sewing and knitting tasks) was also documented in the minutes (Sub-Committee Minutes, Volume 1, page 117). Indeed, the labor of these girls was prodigious. In one year, according to the General Court, the girls produced more than 188 dozen clouts, 121 dozen shirts and shifts of all sizes, and 101 dozen caps, as well as countless coats, handkerchiefs, aprons, petticoats, sleeves, stays, and sheets, along with mending and laundry (General Court Rough Minutes, Volume 2). The labor of the boys in producing network and other rope and twine brought into the Hospital more than 107 pounds in a year, leading the General Committee to "employ a Person from Bristol to teach the Children the art of Spinning and Preparing of Hemp for Twine, Cordage, & Twine for Harpoon Lines" (General Court Rough Minutes, Volume 2).

In preparing children for their laboring lives, the Governors of the hospital were wary of leading them astray. Their food was plain and their living quarters spartan, and as various tasks were developed for the children, they were scrutinized for appropriateness. *An Account* states that "Manufactures in general seem improper for the Employment of Boys, being likely to incline them to a Way of Life not intended for them; if any are ever made Use of, they must be only such as are simple, and laborious, as spinning and twisting Thread and small Ropes, or the like" (*An Account* 69; Levene 59). This idea of inclining boys "to a Way of life not intended for them" was a palpable source of anxiety. The Foundling Hospital functioned as a sealed-off space, with only benefactors and Governors able to move freely outside its walls. At the same time, the children were to be shielded from "negative" influences that might enter; children were to be kept at a distance from anyone who might complicate the constant lessons on gratitude toward benefactors and humility and hard work as supreme values. The Sub-Committee Minutes for May 1755 ordered that "the Porter do not suffer Footmen, menial Servnts or mean and vulgar People, to come into this Hospital ... the Servants of Persons coming to visit the Hospital, as well as their Equipages, be desired to wait without the Gates of the Hospital, till called for by their Master ... and not be permitted to have any Communication with the Children" (Sub-Committee Minutes, Volume 2, page 22). The world of the children was to be controlled and managed in the walled and ordered space of the Hospital grounds, and any dissenting or querulous voices that might undermine the grandness of the patrons were to be avoided at all costs.

The Chapel

Benefactors could observe the children on various occasions; they were sometimes present at the separation of infants from their mothers and they watched the children at work and play on the Hospital grounds. The children were perhaps most visible, however, in Sunday worship at the chapel (Berry 42, 76,

133; McClure 50, 72). Sundays were thus occupied by religious services that had a double function for the foundlings; they were to engrain a sense of Christian virtue in the children, but they were also to reinforce their lesser place in the world relative to their benefactors. The Sub-Committee Minutes from April 1749 explain the ways the religious meeting reinforced the work of the Hospital more generally:

> the Children ... attend divine Service in the Chapel on Sundays, and ... the Officers &c. of the Hospital do often remind them of the lowness of their Condition, that they may early imbibe the Principles of Humility and Gratitude to their Benefactors, and to learn to undergo with Contentment the most servile and laborious Offices; for notwithstanding the innocence of the Children, yet as they are exposed and abandoned by their Parents, they ought to submit to the lowest stations, and should not be educated in such a manner as may put them upon a level with the Children of Parents who have the Humanity and Virtue to preserve them, and Industry to Support them. (Sub-Committee Minutes, Volume 1, page 29)

In fact, this formulation was so central to the Hospital that the recommendation was that this, along with the guidelines for the kinds of trades children were to be trained for, be widely distributed: "they should be published in the London Gazeteer and a Thousand of them printed for the Hospital on Papers without Stamps, and fit to hang up" (Sub-Committee Minutes, Volume 1, page 29). The assumptions of the institution were clear; the children should understand that their position in life was to remain lowly, as they had been abandoned by their heartless parents and saved from a terrible fate only by the generosity of their benefactors. The presumption was that there was something innately wrong with parents who would leave their children with the institution, and while the children should not be expected to pay for the sins of their parents, at the same time, they should understand themselves as having a lesser status than children whose parents exhibited the "humanity," "virtue," and "industry" to take care of their own offspring. They were to repay their care by taking on "the most servile and laborious Offices" and submitting to "the lowest stations."

The chapel, which was finally completed in 1754, was one of the most consistent spaces in which children interacted (even at a distance) with their benefactors, and Sunday services included songs performed in unison by the children (see Figure 6). The assumptions embedded within this music are especially powerful when we consider that the songs were sung by the children to an audience of benefactors and agents of the Foundling Hospital so that through these performances both the children and the benefactors internalized and reinforced the assumptions of the Hospital. The first song, "The Foundling's Hymn" (*Hymns and Songs* 1; Levene 115), lays out the assumptions

Figure 6 Foundling Hospital, the chapel. Although this image is from a later period, it does give a good sense of the relationship between benefactors (below) and the foundlings (seated on the upper level behind the minister). Designed and etched by Thomas Rowlandson and Auguste Charles Pugin, published October 1, 1808. The Elisha Whittelsey Collection, The Metropolitan Museum of Art. Object number 59.533.1671(22) www.metmuseum.org/art/collection/search/744450.

undergirding the care and maintenance of each child.[36] Like the children's daily prayers and the instructions to foundlings in the Sub-Committee Minutes, this hymn reinforces themes of gratitude as well as the shame of their abandonment by their parents: "When Parents deaf to Nature's Voice,/ Their helpless Charge forsook;/ Then Nature's God, who heard our Cries,/ Compassion on us took." Parents here are juxtaposed to God as the very antithesis of His goodness; if He is compassionate to children's cries, their parents are deaf to them. If parents forsake their children, God takes them in. The final stanza merges God's goodness with the institution through which, presumably, He works. The

---

[36] Based on Psalm 27, the Foundling Hymn is reprinted in Berry, 135; she too notes the emphasis in this song on "the children's abandonment, reliance upon charity, and God's providence in saving them from certain death."

children plead (in song) "Continue still to hear our Voice,/ When unto thee we Cry;/ And still the Infants Praise receive,/ And still their Wants supply." It is the institution that supplies the wants of the children, and so the alignments are clear: Parents are bad and uncaring (and therefore ungodly) while the institution and its benefactors do God's work.

This dynamic is made even clearer in a song that celebrates benefactors – "A Hymn" (Hymns and Songs 6–7). Here the birth parents are entirely absent, and the only relationship that matters is between God and the benefactors, with the humble foundlings as intercessors in that relationship: "Father of Mercy hear our Pray'rs,/ For those who do us Good;/ Whose Love for us a place prepares;/ And kindly give us Food." The second stanza makes the connection between God's work and the benefactors explicit: "Each Hand and Heart that lend us Aid,/ Thou dost inspire and guide;/ Nor is their Bounty unrepaid,/ Who for the Poor, the Poor provide." The fourth stanza makes the relationship between God, the foundlings, and the benefactors starkly clear: "For those whose Goodness founded this,/ A better House prepare;/ Receive them to thy heav'nly Bliss,/ And may we meet Them there." It is the salvation of the benefactors that matters, and the foundlings are secondary to that. The "better House" is prepared for the benefactors, not the children, although the children "may" meet them there (if all goes well).

In this hymn, the foundlings sing of their love and gratitude for their benefactors, assuring them that their good deeds align them with God and heaven. The absence of the parents makes the generosity of the benefactors clearer: "Those who do us good" are notably *not* their own parents, but the benevolent strangers to whom these songs are sung. Their generosity in feeding and housing the foundlings echoes God's love, and their care of "the poor" and "the HELPLESS" (second and sixth stanzas) has earned them the prayers and eternal gratitude of the foundlings who sing to them. Again, this hymn emphasizes the vast distance between the foundlings who receive the beneficence and those wealthy benefactors who support them.

The pleasure in watching uniformed children singing in unison not only about their parents' cruelty, but also of the generosity of their benefactors was echoed in many aspects of the institution. In addition to the chapel, the grounds of the Hospital were a park where wealthy people could watch the children work and live their virtuous lives as a testament to their generosity (McClure 72). Benefactors could pay to watch foundlings at work and even buy products of their labor in the gift shop (Berry 133). The children were perpetually on display, and they dutifully performed for benefactors; their performance was of docile, hardworking beings remarkable for their uniformity, not their individuality, to be admired alongside the art and music.

Benefactors intersected with the institution in the great big halls and at public performances (Berry 77), or while viewing the grand paintings (Berry 75) in ornate spaces where they met (Berry 70–71), conferred, and made decisions. Benefactors reveled in their own munificence by observing key moments in the life of the institution, from the reception day when mothers gave up their babies, to children singing in the chapel, to children honing their skills as lowly workers in the parklike setting of the hospital grounds. Each was a source of melancholy enjoyment in which the benefactors congratulated themselves on their intervention in the lives of those they identified as clearly lesser than themselves (Berry 42–44). As the elite explored the loss and suffering of others, they reinforced their own superiority (McClure 50).

The very grand public spaces were quite different from the private quarters where the foundlings lived, and as Helen Berry points out, "to the modern eye, the juxtaposition of opulence in the spaces where the Foundling Hospital's rich patrons gathered, and strict austerity in the children's dormitories and communal areas, is almost obscene" (71). Whatever they were for the foundlings who lived there, for benefactors the Hospital buildings were a pleasant rural escape from the city with a towering central structure (the chapel) as a monument to social relations in which wealthy people extended themselves as far as they were willing to the poor (see Figure 7). That is, the charity that undergirded the institution was about ensuring that the distance between the objects of charity and their benefactors was clearly demarcated, and the formal public spaces operated in relation to the dreariness of the foundlings' experience. The Governors' records inadvertently reveal this relationship, moving dizzyingly from discussions of plain fare for the children and its attendant costs (Sub-Committee Minutes, Volume 2, page 8) to dazzling menus for charity benefits (Sub-Committee Minutes, Volume 2, page 25).

From the songs in the chapel to the rigid schedule and all the preparations for apprenticeships, the children were perpetually reminded of their anticipated class status. Throughout was a constant reminder of the weakness of their parents by whom they had been abandoned. The Hospital regularly reinforced the core principle that as foundlings they were unloved, and as the offspring of uncaring parents, their own impulses and desires were to be drummed out of them. They were to follow instructions, not to think for themselves. Most importantly, they were to understand the web of obligations they were under. If they followed the rules of the Foundling Hospital, they had the possibility of living good lives.

The story some of the tokens tell of loving, grieving parents forced into parting with their children is erased, and a different one takes its place. The children's obligations are to the benefactors, and the first and most important one is to reject their parents and truly see themselves as objects of charity.

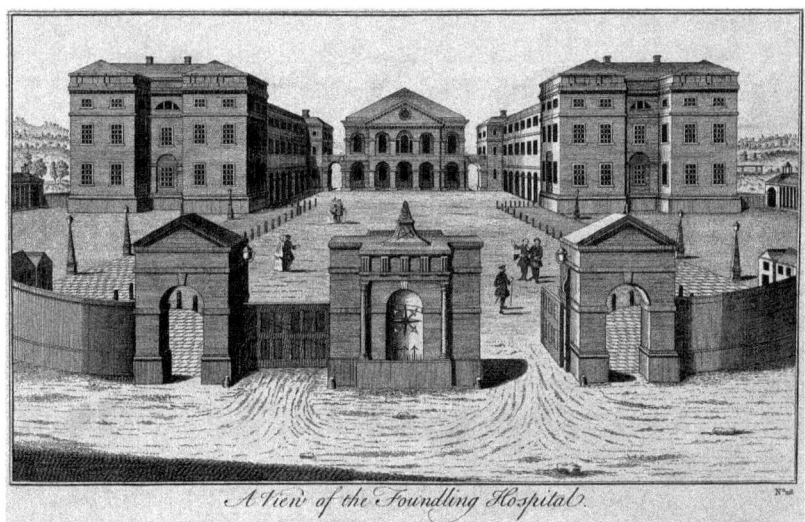

Figure 7 The Foundling Hospital, Holborn, London: A bird's-eye view of the courtyard, with the chapel in the center. Note the absence of children in this view as the grounds are represented as a site of leisure for the gentlemen and ladies depicted here. Engraving by B. Cole, 1754 [after P. Fourdrinier, 1742]. **Source:** Wellcome Collection.

Apprenticeships

By December 1749, there was increasing focus on systematizing and setting up regulations for apprenticeships as the oldest children were nearing the age for such arrangements (Sub-Committee Minutes, Volume 1, page 50). This was to be the culmination of the Foundling Hospital enterprise, the successful completion of the broader mission of transmuting unwanted children into successful laborers. The boys were to be prepared for service on ships or in farming, while the girls were to serve primarily as household servants, and as we have seen, the work arrangements in the institution were geared toward preparing children for this labor (*An Account* 71–72; Levene 61). Apprenticeship Registers reveal that for roughly the first decade or so (the first apprenticeship was initiated in 1751) the boys went as planned into "sea service" and husbandry. This was very much the intention made explicit both in *An Account* and in the Sub-Committee Minutes, and at least initially this very limited role for boys was maintained, although after 1757 there was a significantly expanded set of opportunities for the boys, from peruke maker to apothecary, cheesemonger, watchmaker, jeweler, stationer, and even goldsmith, with a few boys going into household service (Apprenticeship Register, Volume 1, pages 8 through 11). The girls were apprenticed into a variety of households as maids, but perhaps engaging in some capacity in various trades such as silk dyer, smith, shopkeeper, apothecary, bookseller, peruke maker, jeweler, musician, and dyer.[37]

Children received into the institution before the General Reception period came of age in a very different landscape than the later numbers of children passing through the Hospital; while babies were admitted by the hundreds after 1756, older children and their apprenticeship arrangements were still quite individualized before the General Reception babies were old enough to be apprenticed well into the 1760s. The initial arrangements were handled individually; people applied for a child by writing to the Governors or appearing in person with their request. They were vetted by the Governors, and if they were deemed suitable then a formal agreement was signed (Sub-Committee Minutes, Volume 1, page 50). Sometimes potential masters and mistresses asked for specific children by name, but more often they were given whichever child the Governors deemed appropriate. Like the fostering relationships that characterized the first few years of a foundling's life, these apprenticeships could vary from kind and loving to difficult and lonely.

The first child was apprenticed on August 7, 1751, but before that several people asking for a child to work for them had been turned away. Elizabeth Rich, a widow, had asked for a girl in late 1749 (Sub-Committee Minutes, Volume 1, page 50), and William Painter was also turned away a few weeks later after inquiring about apprenticing children for the woolen trade (Sub-Committee Minutes, Volume 1, page 55). Both were told that the children were still too young to go into service at that point. A year and a half later, John Bowles (foundling 5) was apprenticed to Mr Beckingham "in Husbandry" (Sub-Committee Minutes, Volume 1, page 88); Mary Georgia (foundling 93) was the first girl to be apprenticed on August 19, 1752, more than a year after John Bowles (Apprenticeship Register, Volume 1, page 1). She went into the family of John Osmond, a silk dyer, who after much inquiry was "esteem'd & reckon'd humane" by the Governors of the Hospital (Sub-Committee Minutes, Volume 1, page 148). Even William Cadogan, author of *An Essay upon Nursing*, took in an eleven-year-old foundling in 1760: Thomasin Gilling, number 470, "to be imployed in Household Service" (Apprenticeship Register, Volume 1, page 14).

Most children were bound out between ten and twelve years old, although some were older, having worked for some years in the Hospital, and some were considerably younger. For example, child 1528, known at the Hospital as Humphrey Steele (a note with his billet states that he was baptized Richard

---

[37] Only later were children employed in manufacture, a decidedly more challenging situation, especially for some of the girls. See McClure 124–27.

Plummer before coming to the Hospital, [Billet 1528, Billet Book 9]), was "apprenticed" at four years old (Apprenticeship Register, Volume 1, page 14), which seems appalling until we recognize that this arrangement connected him more permanently to his nurse's family (Nursery Book, Volume 1). In fact, the Apprentice Register folds in a number of different kinds of relationships; tucked in among the lists of children apprenticed out to various masters and mistresses is a list that is about a dozen pages long of children returned to their parents from the mid 1750s through the 1780s. Along with the name and address of the parent or relative to whom the child is returned are details such as their employment, which ranged from shoemaker, day laborer, servant, carpenter, journeyman silver buckle maker, watchmaker, and musician to the ubiquitous women's roles of wife, spinster, widow (Apprenticeship Register, Volume 1, pages 301 through 314, pages 329 through 331). Just as was the case for masters and mistresses, inquiries were made into the suitability of the parental figure. From the perspective of the Hospital, this was a relationship to be brokered much as an apprenticeship was; the Hospital was to ascertain the reliability of the adult entering the relationship to ensure that the Hospital's obligations to its foundlings were appropriately met. Like any candidate applying for a child laborer, parents could be rejected by the Hospital for not having the resources or recommendations required.

The Governors took the work of sending children out very seriously in the first few years, carefully vetting individuals and making sure that children were appropriately matched based on their skills and age. In October 1751, the principles of child placement were once again spelled out: "Boys are principally intended for Sailors & Husbandry, and the Girls for Servants in Families." At the same time, the committee concluded, "we ought to have an Eye to-wards the placing them, if need be, and occasion offers, in other Employments ... with respect to the Boys, their Health, Make, Genius, and Disposition should be attended to" just as for the girls attention should be given to "their abilities, Health & Strength" (Sub-Committee Minutes, Volume 1, page 106). In July 1752, when the Sub-Committee agreed to Mary Georgia's apprenticeship (Sub-Committee Minutes, Volume 1, page 148), they did a full accounting of the children on the premises, deciding that ten of the boys were essential to the work of the Hospital, while eleven were available to be placed out "if reputable Persons offer." As for the girls, "the immediate Service of ye Hospital so much requires their Work, that it is the Opinion of this Committee, there are only Two that can as yet be spared," one of whom was already slated for apprenticeship (Sub-Committee Minutes, Volume 1, page 149). The minutes then list sixteen girls and their work, largely sewing and kitchen work, except for the last three, who are relegated to purse making, "having bad Eyes" (Sub-Committee Minutes, Volume 1, page 150).

Woven throughout the minutes for the next few years are requests for children, the examination of the qualities of the person submitting the request, and the constant tally of the needs of the Hospital against the possibility of placing children in good situations. When mariner Henry Bird Jr. was approved for a boy, he "attended the Committee ... and fixed upon Thomas Coram, to take as an Apprentice for the Sea Service, desiring that he might be delivered to him in a few Days, as the Ship wherein he was to be put was ready to sail" (Sub-Committee Minutes, Volume 1, page 198). In 1754. Mr. Trant of York requested both a boy and a girl from the Hospital as apprentices: "having been at ye Hospital, since his coming up, and pitch'd upon James Martin, No. 3, & Sarah Richmond, No. 12," the committee agreed to his choice (Sub-Committee Minutes, Volume 1, page 251). By January 1756, thirty-two children were ready to be placed out in apprenticeships; three boys and two girls remained from the first year (1741), having served the Hospital for their fourteen years while the largest group of both boys and girls ready for service was from the year 1746, making them only ten years old (Sub-Committee Minutes, Volume 2, page 61).

For most children, the apprenticeship was the closing relationship brokered by the hospital; for many of them, it was the final notation in the General Register, akin from the Hospital's perspective to death as it was recorded in the last column for each child titled "Death or final Discharge when reported." It seems to have been very different from the fostering relationship, although certainly overlapping in its intentions. Each child was sent out to apprentice, an arrangement coordinated between the institution and the master or mistress and carefully documented in the official indenture contracts, which are still available in The London Archive but were not digitized. Some are cut in patterns at the top, others are straight; all are formal, elegant affairs, a legal arrangement on the part of the Hospital with the master/mistress. The formality of the document sometimes masked more poignant details; some of these children were only eleven years old, and more than a few of the masters or mistresses couldn't sign their own names. The child is, as is typical in apprenticeships, the *object* being exchanged, not a full signatory. With the wax seal of the Foundling Hospital and the signatures of the Governors, the indentures elaborated the reach of the Foundling Hospital; each was an oversized parchment document filled out in formal handwriting and marked with the imprint of the Hospital (with its ornate figures and big word "Help"). By June 1754, however, they were regularized into a printed form, with blanks for the names of the various individuals and far less elaboration.[38]

---

[38] These apprenticeship indentures are in boxes at The London Archive: one bundle from 1751–53 (A/FH/A/12/003/001-005) and the other from 1754 (A/FH/A/12/004/002).

The training of each foundling in the Hospital was designed to keep their ambitions modest and their fates humble. As they left the hospital for this final assignment the children were given a form filled out with the details of their specific indenture (dates, names, etc.), as well as parting words of wisdom from the institution (McClure, 263–64). The children were reminded one last time of their lowly status and of their obligation to the institution that raised them: "You were taken into it very young, quite helpless, forsaken & deserted by Parents & Friends. Out of Charity have you been fed, clothed, and instructed; which many have wanted" (McClure 263). If their parents (they are reminded) forsook them, the institution did right by them.

> You have been taught to fear God, to love Him, to be honest, careful, laborious, and diligent. ... Be not ashamed that you were bred in this Hospital. Own it; and say that it was thro' the good Providence of Almighty God that you were taken care of. Bless Him for it; and be thankful to those worthy Benefactors who have contributed towards your Maintenance & Support. (McClure 263)

In these final words to the children, the institution reminded them of their obligation to their benefactors. They were to live lives of gratitude and unending duty.

More specifically, the Hospital instructs each child, "You are to behave honestly, justly, soberly, and carefully in every thing, to everybody, and especially towards your [blank] and Family; and to execute all lawful Commands with Industry, Chearfulness, and good Manners. (McClure 263). The instructions conclude:

> As you hope for Success in this World, and Happiness in the next, you are to be mindful of what has been taught you. ... If you follow the Instructions which have all along been taught you, and which we now give you, you may be happy; otherwise you will bring upon yourself Misery, Shame, and Want." (McClure 264)

If the Hospital has offered them every opportunity to be a good and upstanding person, any behavior to the contrary falls on them. The possibility of "Misery, Shame, and Want," precisely the conditions attached in all the Hospital language to the children's parents, is something they must reject but that hovers in their background. The message is clear; children – even (or perhaps especially) those "maintained and educated" by the Hospital – are volatile creatures, needing constant supervision and control. That some children succeeded far beyond the expectations of the institution is a testament to the strength of will some of these children maintained, and the countless variations in their paths along the way through this intensely scrutinized childhood.

Conclusion

The official texts of the Foundling Hospital provide a fascinating account of the ways childhood and citizenship were structured through an institution rather than a family, with men taking the lead in reimagining "the maintenance and education of ... children." When read in tandem with the billet system and the notes and other tokens left with children, as well as other internal records of the hospital, the story becomes far more complicated. Close reading of different kinds of texts and the juxtaposition of various archival materials to each other make visible an extraordinary moment in eighteenth-century London and its implications for the British Empire more generally. The digital archive at the center of this project make that work possible for all readers.

Within ten years of its founding, *An Account* proudly proclaimed "there has already been more than 500 Children received and maintained by this Corporation" (*An Account*, 1749 xviii), a number that was to expand significantly in the decades to come. This was a complicated metric, however, since most of those children were out in the country and by 1749, only a few of those children would have been old enough to return to the Hospital in London – especially when the age of return was raised to five rather than three. In fact, the Sub-Committee Minutes of February 15, 1748, give a list of the children currently living at the Hospital: only thirty-seven boys and forty girls in the grand buildings still under completion (Sub-Committee Minutes, Volume 1, page 21).[39] As modest as these numbers were relative to the ambitions of the Hospital, as an experiment in mass child-rearing, the institution was a powerful force in cultural change. The Foundling Hospital was designed to transform infants into workers, transmuting them from "unwanted" to "useful" on what was expected to be an ever-expanding scale.

The attraction for the institution that took them in is what makes these children so impenetrable for the modern scholar; they were too young to have their own memories or to speak for themselves at the moment of disconnection from their birth situation. As infants, they were to become truly creatures of benevolence, subjects in an experiment in which they had no say. The evidence of their "pre-foundling" existence – their individuated clothes, names, and other forms of identity – were stripped from them and sealed away. Even so, through the fragmentary evidence of the tokens, we see a tension between what the institution wants for them – what the Cadogan text and *An Account* so clearly outline as a pleasing homogeneity – and the mark(s) of their parents. Mothers attempted to speak for and to their children, producing for them a past and

---

[39] Fewer than 150 children lived in the Foundling Hospital at any one time before the 1750s (McClure 76).

a connection to a possible future that is sealed into the billet and replaced with a number.

By redefining parenthood as a series of exchanges and financial transactions, the Foundling Hospital undertook the mass production of citizens, an ambitious project of national pride and optimism around the malleability and reproducibility of citizens. There was a lot to manage; children had to be cared for well over a decade after the original admission date, and then there was at least another decade of managing the indenture and ensuring that the apprenticeship went smoothly (which it didn't always, for a variety of reasons). For children unable to work (through physical or other incapacity), the Hospital committed to lifelong care. Others stayed at the Hospital as gardeners or domestic workers long after their terms as foundlings had expired.

One sign of the complexity of the commitment becomes visible in the comparison of the General Register to the Apprenticeship Registers. The General Register is an orderly numerical list of every child admitted into the Foundling Hospital, ten children per page, with occasional notations for each child for every aspect of her/his life in relation to the institution: inoculation date, nursing placement, apprenticeship placement, and the final discharge from the hospital. Each child's life is encapsulated in a few brief sentences, with notations in different handwriting marking the intervening years between each comment. For the unluckiest children, the comment is brief: a death date within days or a few years of their initial reception at the Hospital. For others, the various phrases that encapsulate the foundling's experience crowd the rectangular space left for such updates. And yet for all the stories and difficulties and complexities of those lived lives, from the perspective of the Hospital, order reigns; children are listed as they were admitted, and they are easily found through their identifying number.

The Apprenticeship Registers are a very different affair, and perhaps a good indicator of the relationship between records and lives, and the ways the Foundling Hospital's order applied to infants, but rarely to the individuals they became as they developed their own personhood – the kind of personhood their mothers had so desperately tried to imagine for them. Despite a valiant effort toward order, the Apprenticeship Registers are jumbled and chaotic, revealing the problem of how to document children – really young adults – at this final stage of their relationship with the Hospital. Through the apprenticeship, the ideal of regimentation breaks down; individual children had talents and inhibitions, limitations and opportunities that set them apart from each other and shifted them in this final step toward adulthood from "objects" of charity back to individuals with their own paths through life.

While the General Registers follow a neatly prescribed numerical order, the Apprenticeship Registers are less dependent on the number and instead are organized in the order children were apprenticed, which was very different for each child. While the child's number is still listed, the Register primarily recognizes the name of the child and apprenticeship agreement, sometimes more than one for any individual child. However, this chronological listing is prefaced by an attempted organization that is alphabetical by the last name of the child – the only possible structure that makes the book searchable since children were put out to apprenticeship as such opportunities arose and at least partially based on the (presumed) talents and abilities of individual children. Numbers could not organize children bound out at different times and at different ages and in different places.

The attempt at order nearly engulfs the actual information; the first third of the book is an alphabetical index that lists each child's name and the page number on which the full record exists. However, the indexes keep collapsing; there is not enough room under certain letters to keep track of all the children. Even the title acknowledges the impossibility of imposing order on this mass of individuals and their comings and goings (see Figure 8):

> Alphabet N° 1 of Book of Children Disposed of, from the 7th of August 1751 inclusive, to the 7th of September 1768 inclusive or to Page 176 part included. NOTE. There is another Alphabet at the End of this Book. (Apprenticeship Register, Volume 1)

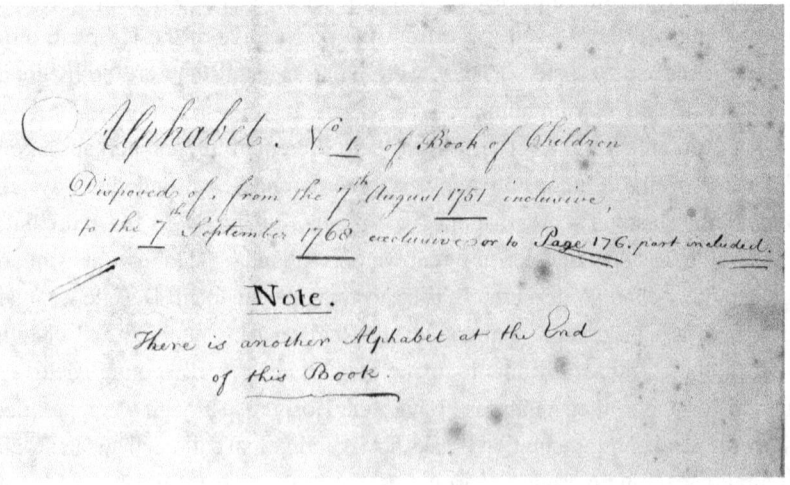

Figure 8 The title page of the first apprenticeship register [A-FH-A-12-003-001-007].

Source: Coram Foundation

In fact, alphabets are disbursed throughout; the first alphabet proceeds through Letter "E" before a random column of the letter "B" is inserted (Apprenticeship Register, Volume 1), and then a few pages later a random column of the letter "C" (Apprenticeship Register, Volume 1) appears, and so on. The children's names spill into corners and the instructions for finding them are nearly hopeless; the second alphabet mentioned on the title page is separate from the additional letter-columns disbursed in the first alphabet, and so while the initial section of the first book gestures at order, in fact finding an individual child's name is challenging.

When the actual list of apprenticeships begins (Apprenticeship Register, Volume 1, page 1) the suggestion of order is tenuous at best. The first indenture began on August 7, 1751, and the book does not indicate whether the terms of this first apprenticeship were completed, although further down the page the list of children's names starts to unravel; the child Mary How changes from one apprenticeship to another, and the language blends and crosses over so that it is difficult to see where her record ends and that of the next child, Samuel Taylor, begins. And so it goes throughout the book, with details of apprenticeships agreed to, assigned, broken, and reconfigured listed as if these lives can be ordered and managed in neat little columns.

As noted earlier, tucked among the pages is the list of children returned to their parents, only slightly differentiated from the rest of the apprenticeships listed in the Register (Apprenticeship Register, Volume 1, pages 301–14). At the top of several pages are the calculations, the cumulative weight of children dispersed back to their parents over the decades from the 1750s through the 1770s. The thirteen from the first page are carried over to the second, with the totals carefully tallied: 26 jumps to 39, 78, 91 and then 104 (before the tally gets abandoned even as the list continues). These are the lucky few, the rare children among the thousands who entered the Hospital who found their way back to their birth families. The Apprenticeship Register adds their names, making their relationships visible, but the "Book of Children Disposed of" does not acknowledge the vast difference between the financial arrangement that is an apprenticeship and the return of a child to her/his parents.

Each of the 1,384 infants received into the Foundling Hospital before the start of the General Reception period in June 1756 was individualized through a billet and a numbered entry into the General Register; beyond that children were variously documented in other places depending on their needs and circumstances. The Sub-Committee Minutes, the records that most closely summarized the concerns of the Governors, tended to engage with children as categories rather than individuals: children at the Hospital or infants in the country, children ready to return to the Hospital from the countryside, or infants

Figure 9 Coram's Fields, park entry. The juxtaposition of the modern policy with the still extant entry of the original Foundling Hospital grounds is striking. **Source:** author's photograph.

to be transported by nurses elsewhere. Clothing was needed for different age groups and some foods needed to be purchased as opposed to what could be produced on site. Certainly there were exceptions: John Herbert was examined by the Governors because of his unusual feet ("by reason of him being crump-footed"), and they concluded he needed individually fitted shoes (Sub-Committee Minutes, Volume 1, page 111). Swiss Lambert's "humour" required him to stay in the country until it could be resolved, according to a letter from the inspectress to the Governors (Sub-Committee Minutes, Volume 1, page 157), while Hester Yargrove's "Scrophulous Humour" elicited extended discussion and consultation with several doctors (Sub-Committee Minutes, Volume 1, pages 165 and 166). Thomas Dingley was a "weakly child" while Ann Froggat was "an ideot & subject to Fits," which meant that their individual circumstances had to be discussed by the gentlemen Governors (Sub-Committee

Minutes, Volume 1, page 193). Other children's names are scattered throughout the minutes, a reminder of the human beings passing through the institution, although the records documenting the lived experiences of the actual children are sparse; brief comments are marked in the General Register, and passing references are in various committee minutes. We know very little of the marriages, births, misfortunes, and joys that these children went on to encounter, and there is very little evidence from the earliest years that has survived beyond their infant records. In this way, the archive marks a very particular kind of childhood, an experiment in development rather than full personhood.

The Foundling Hospital as an institution defined the terms through which children could be turned into productive laborers, servants to the benevolent class that had saved them. The structures and organizing principles of the Foundling Hospital shaped much of what was to come in the colonial world; by establishing ways of thinking about charity, benevolence, and the proper treatment of children, this institution shaped such spaces throughout the British Empire. The texts from the opening years of the Foundling Hospital make explicit the expectation that for children to become upstanding members of the Commonwealth, they were to accept their secondary status and remain humble and grateful. Whether they actually lived within these expectations or defied the odds is largely invisible to us today. In a world shaped by texts, rules, and seemingly endless documentation, the lives of these children moved in very different directions, and their experiences defied easy categorization.

Figure 10 Coram's Fields, side view.
Source: author's photograph.

Today the site of the former Foundling Hospital is largely given over to Coram Fields, designated as a "children only park" with the tag line "a safe place for all children" (https://coramsfields.org). A vibrant and bustling place, the park hosts activities and events geared to children, and in fact the grounds are accessible for adults only in the company of its true guests, children under sixteen years of age (see Figure 9). On a typical day, the shouts of children playing games or swinging in the playground are a striking contrast to the gates and outer buildings still standing from the original site, even though the main buildings are long gone. The bright toys and implements of a modern daycare are visible under the still extant seal of the Foundling Hospital on the front of one of the side buildings, and the long outer buildings flank the park just as they did in the original etchings of the site (see Figure 10). Through this juxtaposition we are reminded of the long arm of institutional policies and structures, as benevolent as their intentions may have been, in establishing our modern assumptions about childhood and charity, and we are well served in remembering the ways those before us lived out their principles in ways that, whether we like it or not, are still all around us.

Works Cited

Primary Sources

A Sketch of the General Plan for Executing the General Purposes of the Royal Charter, Establishing an Hospital for the Maintenance and Education of Exposed and Deserted Children; as Reported by the Gentlemen Desired to Consider of a General Plan, for Executing the Charity, to the Committee for Transacting the Affairs of the Hospital, on the 16th of July, 1740. London: printed by John Baskett, Printer to the King's most Excellent Majesty, 1740. bit.ly/45XEOlf.

An Account of the Hospital for the Maintenance and Education of Exposed and Diserted [sic] Young Children. In Which Is the Charter, Act of Parliament, Bylaws and Regulations of the Said Corporation. By Order of the Governors of the Said Hospital. London: n.p., 1749. bit.ly/468Wnjs. Also cited from Alysa Levene, ed. *Narratives of the Poor in Eighteenth-Century Britain*. Vol. 3. London: Pickering & Chatto, 2006. Pp. 5–64.

Cadogan, William. *An Essay upon Nursing, and the Management of Children, from Their Birth to Three Years of Age. By a Physician. In a Letter to One of the Governors of the Foundling Hospital. Published by Order of the General Committee for Transacting the Affairs of the Said Hospital.* London: printed for J. Roberts in Warwick-Lane, 1748. bit.ly/45EIIAA. Also cited from Alysa Levene, ed. *Narratives of the Poor in Eighteenth-Century Britain*. Vol. 3. London: Pickering & Chatto, 2006. Pp. 93–112.

Coram's Foundling Hospital Archive,1739–1899. These digitized records, now closed to the public, are housed in The London Archive (TLA) and owned by the Coram Foundation. https://archives.coram.org.uk/records/CFH

The digital records consulted for this project are organized as follows:

Administration: Minutes, 1739–1895
  General Court Rough Minutes, Volumes 1 and 2
  Daily Committee Minutes and House Committee Minutes
  Sub-Committee Minutes, Volumes 1 and 2
https://archives.coram.org.uk/records/CFH/A/03

Administration: Secretary's Records: Admission and Discharge of Children, 1741–1880
  Billet Books, Volumes 1–18
  General Register, Volume 1
https://archives.coram.org.uk/records/CFH/A/09

Administration: Secretary's Records: Children in the Country, 1749–1812
  Nursery Book, Volume 1
  Inspections Book, Volume 1
  Register of Children sent to Shrewsbury
  https://archives.coram.org.uk/records/CFH/A/10
Administration: Secretary's Records: Children Claimed, 1758–1796
  Register of Children Claimed
  Petitions Claiming Children, Volume 5
  https://archives.coram.org.uk/records/CFH/A/11
Administration: Secretary's Records: Apprenticing, 1751–1899
  Apprenticeship Register, Volume 1
  https://archives.coram.org.uk/records/CFH/A/12
Administration: Secretary's Records: Chapel, 1741–1885
  Baptism and Burial Register
  https://archives.coram.org.uk/records/CFH/A/14
Foundling Hospital, undigitized. The London Archive.
  A/FH/A/06/001/002 Anonymous Letter relating to "the Management of Children according to Dr Cadogan's Scheme and Book"
  A/FH/A/12/004/001 Apprenticeship Indentures 1751–1753
  A/FH/A/12/004/002 Apprenticeship Indentures, 1754
"Instructions to Apprentices" printed as Appendix IV in Ruth McClure, *Coram's Children: The London Foundling Hospital in the Eighteenth Century.* New Haven: Yale University Press, 1981.
Psalms, Hymns and Anthems for the Use of the Children of the Hospital for the Maintenance and Education of Exposed and Deserted Young Children. 1765. https://wellcomecollection.org/works/nzqhw9qh.
The Report of the General Committee for Directing . . . and Transacting the Business . . . of the Corporation of the Governors and Guardians of the Hospital for the Maintenance . . . of Exposed and Deserted Young Children. London: printed by J. Baskett, 1740. bit.ly/4mBFaFr.

Secondary Sources

Andrew, Donna T. *Philanthropy and Police: London Charity in the Eighteenth Century.* Princeton: Princeton University Press, 2014.

Ariès, Philippe. *Centuries of Childhood: A Social History of Family Life.* New York: Vintage Books, 1962.

Berry, Helen. *Orphans of Empire: The Fate of London's Foundlings.* Oxford: Oxford University Press, 2019.

Bright, Janette and Gillian Clark. *Introduction to the Tokens at the Foundling Museum*. London: Foundling Museum, 2000.

Brooks, Joanna. *Why We Left: Untold Stories and Songs of America's First Immigrants*. Minneapolis: University of Minnesota Press, 2013.

Brownlow, John. *The History and Objects of the Foundling Hospital, with a Memoir of the Founder*. As Revised by W. S. Wintle, Secretary, 1881. Wellcome Collection, 1881. https://wellcomecollection.org/works/zeyxmz7m.

Clark, Gillian and Janette Bright. "The Foundling Hospital and Its Token System." *Family & Community History* 18, no. 1 (April 1, 2015): 53–68. https://doi.org/10.1179/1463118015Z.00000000039.

Cohen, Michael. "Addison, Blake, Coram, and the London Foundling Hospital: Rhetoric as Philanthropy and Art." *The Centennial Review* 34, no. 4 (1990): 540–66.

Compston, Herbert Fuller Bright. *Thomas Coram: Churchman, Empire Builder and Philanthropist*. London: Society for Promoting Christian Knowledge, 1918.

Cowan, Justine. *The Secret Life of Dorothy Soames: A Memoir*. New York: Harper, an imprint of HarperCollins, 2021.

Evans, Tanya. *Unfortunate Objects: Lone Mothers in Eighteenth-Century London*. Houndmills: Palgrave Macmillan, 2005.

Farge, Arlette. *The Allure of the Archives*. The Lewis Walpole Series in Eighteenth-Century Culture and History. New Haven: Yale University Press, 2013.

Fuentes, Marisa Joanna. *Dispossessed Lives: Enslaved Women, Violence, and the Archive*. 1st ed. Early American Studies. Philadelphia: University of Pennsylvania Press, 2016.

Gibson, Kate. "Fostering the Foundlings." *History Today* 73, no. 4 (April 2023): 30–37.

Hartman, Saidiya. *Scenes of Subjection: Terror, Slavery, and Self-Making in Nineteenth-Century America*. Revised and updated 25th anniversary ed. New York: W. W. Norton, 2022.

Hartman, Saidiya. "Venus in Two Acts." *Small Axe: A Journal of Criticism* 12, no. 2 (2008): 1–14. https://doi.org/10.1215/-12-2-1.

Johnston, Elizabeth. "Big Mother: Breastfeeding Rhetoric and the Panopticon in Popular Culture, 1700 to Present." In *Breastfeeding and Culture: Discourses and Representations*, edited by Ann Marie A. Short, Abigail L. Palko, and Dionne Irving, 20–32. Ontario: Demeter Press, 2018.

Levene, Alysa. *Childcare, Health and Mortality at the London Foundling Hospital, 1741–1800: "Left to the Mercy of the World."* Manchester: Manchester University Press, 2012.

———. "The Origins of the Children of the London Foundling Hospital, 1741–1760: A Reconsideration." *Continuity and Change* 18, no. 2 (2003): 201–35. https://doi.org/10.1017/S0268416003004594.

Levene, Alysa, ed. *Narratives of the Poor in Eighteenth-Century Britain*. Vol. 3. London: Pickering & Chatto, 2006.

Lyons, Scott Richard. *X-Marks: Native Signatures of Assent*. Indigenous Americas. Minneapolis: University of Minnesota Press, 2010.

McClure, Ruth K. *Coram's Children: The London Foundling Hospital in the Eighteenth Century*. New Haven: Yale University Press, 1981.

Miles, Tiya. *All That She Carried: The Journey of Ashley's Sack, A Black Family's Keepsake*. New York: Random House, 2021.

Miley, Frances, and Andrew Read. "Go Gentle Babe: Accounting and the London Foundling Hospital, 1757–97." *Accounting History* 21, no. 2–3 (May 1, 2016): 167–84. https://doi.org/10.1177/1032373216644259.

Nixon, Cheryl. *The Orphan in Eighteenth-Century Law and Literature: Estate, Blood, and Body*. Burlington: Ashgate, 2011.

Perry, Ruth. "Colonizing the Breast: Sexuality and Maternity in Eighteenth-Century England." *Journal of the History of Sexuality* 2, no. 2 (1991): 204–34.

Phillips, Claire. "Child Abandonment in England, 1741–1834: The Case of the London Foundling Hospital." *Genealogy* 3, no. 3 (2019). https://doi.org/10.3390/genealogy3030035.

Pinsky, Robert. "The Foundling Tokens." *The American Scholar* 84, no. 3 (2015): 54–56.

Private Virtue and Publick Spirit Display'd. In a Succinct Essay on the Character of Capt. Thomas Coram, Who Deceased the 29th of March, and Was Interr'd in the Chapel of the Foundling Hospital, (a Charity Established by His Solicitation) April 3d, 1751. London: printed for J. Roberts, at the Oxford-Arms, in Warwick-Lane, 1751.

Pugh, Gillian. *London's Forgotten Children: Thomas Coram and the Foundling Hospital*. Stroud: The History Press, 2013.

Ramsland, John. "The London Foundling Hospital and Its Significance as a Child-Saving Institution." *Australian Social Work* 45, no. 2 (June 1, 1992): 23–36. https://doi.org/10.1080/03124079208550132.

Schattschneider, Laura. "The Infants' Petitions: An English Poetics of Foundling Reception, 1741–1837." *Studies in Eighteenth-Century Culture* 33, no. 1 (2004): 71–99. https://doi.org/10.1353/sec.2010.0298.

Shchuka, Virlana M. "'Nursed under His Own Eye': Co-nursing Fathers and the Spectacle of Breastfeeding in the British Romantic Period." *Eighteenth-Century Fiction* 34, no. 4 (2022): 441–69.

Stone, Lawrence. *The Family, Sex and Marriage in England, 1500–1800*. New York: Harper & Row, 1977, Harper, c1977. https://hdl-handle-net.ezproxy.trincoll.edu/2027/heb01414.0001.001.

Styles, John. *The Dress of the People: Everyday Fashion in Eighteenth-Century England*. New Haven: Yale University Press, 2007.

Styles, John. "Objects of Emotion: The London Foundling Hospital Tokens, 1741–60." In *Writing Material Culture History*, edited by Anne Gerritsen and Giorio Riello, 165–71. London: Bloomsbury Academic, 2015.

Styles, John. *Threads of Feeling: The London Foundling Hospital's Textile Tokens, 1740–1770*. London: Foundling Museum, 2010.

Wisecup, Kelly. *Assembled for Use: Indigenous Compilation and the Archives of Early Native American Literatures*. The Henry Roe Cloud Series on American Indians and Modernity. New Haven: Yale University Press, 2021.

Zytaruk, Maria. "Artifacts of Elegy: The Foundling Hospital Tokens." *Journal of British Studies* 54, no. 2 (2015): 320–48.

Acknowledgments

This project emerged from a longer, very differently focused study on early America, and I am indebted to the people along the way who helped shape it and offered encouragement. The first is the Element series editor, Eve Tavor Bannet, whose enthusiasm and patience were essential to seeing this through as a stand-alone publication. Special thanks to Chris Jones and Beck Price at the Coram Foundation. I am indebted to them for sharing their extensive knowledge of the Foundling Hospital's extraordinary archive and their willingness to put me in touch with other scholars. I am also grateful to them for giving me access to these materials at various stages of digitization, and it is no exaggeration to say that this project couldn't have come into being without them. I am also grateful to Lydia Clay-White and Poppy Farr, both Heritage Engagement Interns in 2024 who were wonderfully helpful, and whose close attention to the archive was inspiring. Lynn Cheng and Hope Bettencourt were enthusiastic research assistants through the Public Humanities Collaborative at Trinity College in the summer of 2024, and the manuscript benefited enormously from their painstaking work and thoughtful engagement. Caitlin Kennedy at the Coram Foundation was a most helpful guide through the intricacies of accessing the collection in its transition from The London Archive to its digital form. I am especially grateful for her introduction to the modern incarnation of the institution, so very different from its earliest days even as it maintains a commitment to children and their care. Trinity College (Hartford) supported my research both financially and intellectually: I am grateful to colleagues who engaged with this work and thankful for a generous sabbatical that allowed me to dig into this project. Finally, unending gratitude to my family: James Truman, my partner in life who read the manuscript and offered all kinds of encouragement, and our children, Anna and Cameron Truman-Wyss, who were enthusiastic and engaged listeners as I shared the often heart-wrenching discoveries from the archive.

Permission to reprint images is gratefully acknowledged from the Coram Foundation and the Wellcome Collection as well as the Metropolitan Museum of Art.

Cambridge Elements

Eighteenth-Century Connections

Series Editors
Eve Tavor Bannet
University of Oklahoma

Eve Tavor Bannet is George Lynn Cross Professor Emeritus, University of Oklahoma and editor of *Studies in Eighteenth-Century Culture*. Her monographs include *Empire of Letters: Letter Manuals and Transatlantic Correspondence 1688–1820* (Cambridge, 2005), *Transatlantic Stories and the History of Reading, 1720–1820* (Cambridge, 2011), and *Eighteenth-Century Manners of Reading: Print Culture and Popular Instruction in the Anglophone Atlantic World* (Cambridge, 2017). She is editor of *British and American Letter Manuals 1680–1810* (Pickering & Chatto, 2008), *Emma Corbett* (Broadview, 2011) and, with Susan Manning, *Transatlantic Literary Studies* (Cambridge, 2012).

Markman Ellis
Queen Mary University of London

Markman Ellis is Professor of Eighteenth-Century Studies at Queen Mary University of London. He is the author of *The Politics of Sensibility: Race, Gender and Commerce in the Sentimental Novel* (1996), *The History of Gothic Fiction* (2000), *The Coffee-House: a Cultural History* (2004), and *Empire of Tea* (co-authored, 2015). He edited *Eighteenth-Century Coffee-House Culture* (4 vols, 2006) and *Tea and the Tea-Table in Eighteenth-Century England* (4 vols 2010), and co-editor of *Discourses of Slavery and Abolition* (2004) and *Prostitution and Eighteenth-Century Culture: Sex, Commerce and Morality* (2012).

Advisory Board
Linda Bree, *Independent*
Claire Connolly, *University College Cork*
Gillian Dow, *University of Southampton*
James Harris, *University of St Andrews*
Thomas Keymer, *University of Toronto*
Jon Mee, *University of York*
Carla Mulford, *Penn State University*
Nicola Parsons, *University of Sydney*
Manushag Powell, *Purdue University*
Robbie Richardson, *University of Kent*
Shef Rogers, *University of Otago*
Eleanor Shevlin, *West Chester University*
David Taylor, *Oxford University*
Chloe Wigston Smith, *University of York*
Roxann Wheeler, *Ohio State University*
Eugenia Zuroski, *MacMaster University*

About the Series
Exploring connections between verbal and visual texts and the people, networks, cultures and places that engendered and enjoyed them during the long Eighteenth Century, this innovative series also examines the period's uses of oral, written and visual media, and experiments with the digital platform to facilitate communication of original scholarship with both colleagues and students.

Cambridge Elements

Eighteenth-Century Connections

Elements in the Series

Paratext Printed with New English Plays, 1660–1700
Robert D. Hume

The Art of the Actress
Fashioning Identities

A Performance History of The Fair Penitent
Elaine McGirr

Labour of the Stitch: The Making and Remaking of Fashionable Georgian Dress
Serena Dyer

Early English Periodicals and Early Modern Social Media
Margaret J. M. Ezell

Reading with the Burneys: Patronage, Paratext, and Performance
Sophie Coulombeau

On Wonder: Literature and Science in the Long Eighteenth Century
Tita Chico

The Epistemologies of Progress
Richard Adelman

Networks of Reception in the Eighteenth-Century British Press and Laurence Sterne
Mary Newbould

Restoration Acting and Other Business
David Roberts

Unveiling Lady Scott
Céline Sabiron

The London Foundling Hospital and Eighteenth-Century Objects of Charity: Recovering the Digital Archive
Hilary E. Wyss

A full series listing is available at: www.cambridge.org/EECC

For EU product safety concerns, contact us at Calle de José Abascal, 56–1°, 28003 Madrid, Spain or eugpsr@cambridge.org.

www.ingramcontent.com/pod-product-compliance
Lightning Source LLC
LaVergne TN
LVHW011854060526
838200LV00054B/4330